Walk an Aisle in My Shoes

by

Dave Rackham

Library and Archives Canada Cataloguing in Publication

Rackham, Dave, 1958-
    Walk an Aisle in My Shoes / Dave Rackham

ISBN 978-0-9810170-0-6

1. Grocery trade--Humor. 2. Grocery trade--Employees--Humor.
3. Grocery shopping--Humor. I. Title.

PN6231.G88R32 2008   C818'.602   C2008-903166-0

ISBN 978-0-9810170-0-6

Publisher
Western Spirit Publishing Inc., Calgary, Alberta
drackham@shaw.ca

Project Management
Debbie Elicksen, Freelance Communications, Calgary, Alberta

Design and Production
Lisa-Elaine Arseneault, Sublime Media, Calgary, Alberta

Printing
Friesens, Altona, Manitoba

Front Cover Photo
Wally West, The Exploration Place

Back Cover Photo
Dave Rackham

Walk an Aisle in My Shoes – First Edition
Printed and Bound in Canada
Copyright 2008

Dedication

Walk an Aisle in My Shoes is the sum of the bits and pieces that the people I was so lucky to work with, gave of themselves. If it wasn't for these people making it so interesting and enjoyable to come to work each day, there would be no stories.

Thanks to my family and friends who put up with me reading these stories to them repeatedly (you can all start answering my calls again). If it wasn't for your belief in me, I doubt very much if I would've met the challenges of writing this book.

Lastly, to my late Aunt June, as she was one of my biggest supporters, "God love ya."

Dave Rackham

Acknowledgements

I would like to acknowledge the help provided by Wendy Lukasiewicz from OWL Editing. Trish Pozzo for taking her own time to assist in the early formatting and editing. Special thanks to Jim and Arlis Rackham for their guidance, sound advice and their relentless commitment to making me a better speller. Finally, to the team of Debbie Elicksen of Freelance Communications and Lisa-Elaine Arseneault of Sublime Media for putting the final package together. Your spirit is infectious. To all of you, thank you for helping me take a few ideas and some wishful thinking and turning it into *Walk an Aisle in My Shoes.*

Table of Contents

Prologue

We've all been asked the question, "What do you want to be when you grow up?" You likely said fireman, policeman, doctor, lawyer, astronaut, or even hockey player. I remember using a fear tactic once with my parents and saying, "garbage man." To that they countered, "So long as you're happy." It's likely that you never once said, "I want to be a manager of a grocery store." I can't count the number of times in the store I would hear a parent commenting to their child, "See, you better work hard in school or you could end up here."

The grocery retail industry is very misunderstood. The people who make up the industry aren't given credit for the role they play in your life. After all, you most likely visit us two to three times a week, probably more than you visit your parents. So why is the industry so maligned? I'm sure it doesn't help that the only reference we ever got on television was that mousy, yet lovable, merchant Nels Olsen in *Little House on the Prairie.* I hope this book, achieves some greater understanding from the public about just how dynamic this industry is and give the people that work in it the respect they deserve.

The collections of stories in this book for the most part are simple and humourous. They capture the day-to-day experiences of someone who, like most people in this industry, fell into it. I've built my career and lived my life with the attitude that "My glass isn't just half full, it's frosty too!" Let me share some of the stories that a thirty-one year career in your neighbourhood grocery store can generate. It may not change your life, but you just may see it a little differently after you've 'walked an aisle in my shoes.'

Rise and Shine

It was the summer of 1974 and I had just enjoyed the Canada Day long weekend. For a fifteen year old soon to be sixteen, I had the world by the tail. I was looking forward to the summer: no school, no worries, no nothing. This was the summer I was going to play a little soccer, learn to drive, party with my friends, and meet girls, not necessarily in that order. In other words, I was King of the Carefree!

As a kid growing up in Calgary, Alberta, I was living the typical middle-class life. My family consisted of my mom and dad, one older sister, and two younger brothers. What was not so typical was that each morning, regardless of school or not, the family was required to get up at 7:00 am to have breakfast with Dad. It was important to my dad to have his family around him. I'm not positive, but I think we served as a reminder each morning as to why he should go to work. I know it wasn't for the stimulating conversation. It wasn't until a few years later that he actually let us kids see him for who he was, aside from being our father.

Now, Mom was different when it came to conversing with the kids. Being a stay-at- home mom in the sixties and seventies allowed her to be more comfortable communicating with us. When our cub pack couldn't find anyone to lead it, my mom volunteered to be the "Akela" for the pack. I believe that experience, keeping twenty-five cubs entertained, cultivated the need to keep us all busy. This quality reared its ugly head at one of these breakfasts. Mom made a statement that, at the time, I was unaware of the impact it would have on me.

Eventually it would affect every day for the rest my life. Over a bowl of Froot Loops, it was decided that my sister Susan and I should get a job!

What was this? My sister had already turned seventeen, and she should be looking for a job, but I wasn't even sixteen. I figured I could fall through the cracks until next summer, since I wouldn't be sixteen until July 25.

My mom not only offered the idea of work but also volunteered a suggestion as to where we should apply. A Safeway was being built in the new mall about six blocks away. For a kid that babysat the odd time around the block, this felt like an out of town job! Couldn't I wait to find something a little closer? I knew that fighting it wasn't an option. After the stories my dad had told of the jobs he did as a kid – killing turkeys in a slaughterhouse, roofing houses, and delivering documents on a bicycle in twenty-below weather, all before the age of twelve – I knew I was hooped! My only chance was to apply for the job, but not get hired.

I had a plan! Look scruffy for the interview and give bad answers to whatever questions they threw at me. I knew from school friends that Safeway was very strict on hair length. It was the seventies. My hair wasn't long by those standards, but by Safeway standards? No way, Jose. I planned to show up with long hair, old Levi's, and my favourite T-shirt, accompanied by a well broken-in pair of Basketmasters. I'd give a few quick answers during the interview, if I got that far, and look out summer, here I come!

Growing up, I never appreciated just how sharp my parents were. Little by little my plan fell apart. My mom read every move I made and countered it with a move of her own. First thing that morning I was sent to get a haircut. It had been two months since my last haircut and suddenly today she decided I needed one. No problem, I still had the wardrobe plan in place, until a brown pair of cords and a suitable shirt were selected for me, and the Basketmasters were traded for Hushpuppies.

So, off to apply my sister and I went. I could now only cling to the one part of my plan left: to screw up the interview. Both Susan and I were interviewed at the same time but by two different people. My sister was interviewed by an older lady (later I found out she was the head of Human Resources) and I by a young fellow (who eventually became vice president). He introduced himself as Gord and I introduced myself as Dave. I was asked to tell a little bit about myself. I replied I was going into grade eleven; I play soccer and basketball. The usual stuff. Not much chance to sabotage the interview there. Then it happened.

Gord gave me the "I'm out of here" question on a silver platter: "Why do you want to work for Safeway?" I paused for a moment... my mind reeling with possible answers.

"I heard you paid well." That greedy, self-serving answer should do it. I was ready for the "Thank you, David, don't call us, we'll call you. Next please." But instead I got, "I'm very impressed. You've obviously done your homework. We're very proud of the wages we pay." Then the killer, "Can you start tomorrow?" I was so stunned, all I could say was yes. I was told where to go, when to go, what to wear, and oh yes, get a haircut!

This is how my thirty-one-year career in the grocery retail business started. As reluctant as I was, the retail industry soon became my life and I loved it. It's an industry like no other. Every day was like a snowflake, no two ever being the same. To think that all this started over a bowl of Froot Loops. I sometimes wonder what would have happened if I had chosen Raisin Bran.

My first store; funny I remember it
being busier than this!

Sharp Dressed Man

I had been gainfully employed for about an hour and a half and began to realize I wasn't at all prepared to participate with the daily work force. Besides getting another haircut — the second in two days — I was instructed to be at work with a dress shirt, dress pants, leather shoes (my Hushpuppies didn't make the cut), and a tie! I hadn't worn a tie since the blue striped clip-on bow tie I had worn to Sunday school.

I went out in search of new clothes for my new job. It was 1974 and the freedom to express yourself was not only encouraged, it was your obligation. I went to The Bay to find the exact clothes that would accurately display the inner me. The only problem was I didn't know exactly who or what the inner me was. After less than an hour, I had my new look. Evidently, the inner me was fairly close to the surface.

At home, my mom, her friend and two of her daughters talked me into putting on this new look of mine. With a little reluctance, I came out wearing my new threads. Brown slip-on leather shoes, red, brown and yellow plaid corduroy bell bottom pants (with a cuff), a tight beige polyester shirt with button down pockets, a tight pullover chocolate brown vest and a knitted chocolate brown tie. The women nodded their approval. I had style. I was 'The Man.'

My first shift started at 8:00 am the next morning. What I didn't know was that the doors didn't open until 9:00. How do you get into a closed grocery store? I finally made my way in through an 'out' door on the other side of the store. I was already sweating and I hadn't even begun my shift yet!

I wasn't sure who to see or where to go. All the objects in the store seemed a blur. The workers were all moving fast and with a sense of purpose. I stood motionless, trying to determine where I should be. What I would have given for a sense of purpose. The quick up and down glances I was getting told me I was being carefully checked out. Incredibly, everyone knew it was my first day.

Finally, a man exited a door and headed straight for me. He was balding, a little overweight, wearing a white shirt and tie. He approached me, shaking his head in disgust.

"So you're the new kid, Dave?" I replied, "Yes," relieved that I got the first question right. Obviously this gentleman was the manager. "What the hell are you wearing? This isn't a fashion show!" Apparently plaid bellbottoms were not allowed. My shirt could only be white and the sweater was traded for an apron. Later on I would tell the people I hired that, "If you wouldn't wear the pants anywhere but work, they're probably the right ones."

When I think back to those seventies clothes, I thank God people had the ability to see past them. I learned that it's not the clothes you wear to work that make the man or woman, but how you work in those clothes. The seventies provided us with some painful memories — Watergate, disco, and the Ford Pinto — but nothing was as painful as the clothes they lead us to believe had style.

Educational Television

We all know Barney Fife, the likable, by-the-book, yet inept deputy of Sheriff Andy Taylor. I was always a fan of *The Andy Griffith Show* and particularly a fan of the Barney Fife character. To watch Barney was extremely entertaining. To work with a Barney-like character was sometimes entertaining, but more often, frustrating.

The Barney-type usually held the position of third person, a thankless job somewhere between the assistant manager and the rank and file general clerk. The general clerk or "stock boy" filled the shelves. The third person had the authority of the assistant but the compensation of a clerk. The company used this position to determine if an employee had any potential or leadership ability.

"Barney" was our third person. He had the Don Knotts appearance: about 5'9," weighing an impressive one hundred forty-five pounds, and slightly hunched, most likely caused by carrying the weight of the world on his shoulders. He was always looking to order someone to do something, so long as he got to give the order.

After a while as general clerk, you became very familiar with the job. Unless something extraordinary occurred during the shift, the actual job function was very routine. I had now been working at the store for about four years and had a pretty good grasp of the tasks that were required to be done each shift.

It was a Friday night when Bill, a friend and co-worker and I were in the back room working the specials to replenish the shelves, basically doing the function we did every shift. Now Bill was a very bright individual. He and I had many classes at university together and Bill eventually became a vice president of a multi-national corporation. Of course, at eighteen you're not referred to as a bright individual, but rather as a "smart ass." Once in a while, when sufficiently motivated, Bill fell into that latter category.

That particular night, Barney came into the back room with his chest puffed up, strutting around like a peacock. With his hands placed on his hips, he observed what we were doing, which was loading product on carts to be worked to the shelves. Barney paused for a moment and then in his most "God-like" voice ordered us to do exactly what we were already doing!

While I just shook my head in bewilderment; Bill had a different reaction. He stopped what he was doing, stood his full six foot three inches, looked down into Barney's eyes, paused a moment for effect, and then said, "Barney, fuck off!" Well, Barney was stunned. "You can't say that to me!" Bill, very calmly looked at him again and said, "Barney," another pause for effect, "fuck off!" This second attack sent Barney in search of the store manager. Bill smiled at me like the kid who had just robbed the cookie jar. It was busy up front and we thought we could minimize the inevitable repercussions of Bill's 'minor indiscretion' if we were observed doing the least popular but most needed job of wrapping groceries.

The way the check stands were positioned gave us a theatre-like view into the manager's office through the large picture window facing the front of the store. Bill and I took our places at the check stands. We had a perfect view of Barney, arms flailing about. We couldn't hear them, but we could see them – very similar to a large screen TV, with no sound. The store manager was using his hands in a calming motion, trying to suppress some of the emotion coming from his third person. We could see Barney say, "I want him fired!" We could see the manager pick up the intercom. He had this habit of getting on it before he thought about what he was going to say. "Uh Bill, uh Bill…could you come to the office, please?"

Bill looked at me and said, "If I don't come back, it was good working with you." You see, the store manager was not one you could screw with. Bill was smart enough to know this. Bill's head hung low. If I hadn't been so worried for his well being, I would have shouted, "Dead man walking!" I just didn't have the heart.

Bill was now standing beside Barney, facing the manager. Again, you could see the words. "Bill," the manager said, "did you tell Barney to fuck off?" Bill lifted his head and looked at Barney, and then he looked at the manager with what appeared to be actual remorse. He nodded his head and I could see him say, "Yes, I did."

Bill claims he heard angels singing, and I believe him, because what happened next was just short of a miracle. The manager said, "Bill, you can go." He wasn't fired, he wasn't disciplined, and he wasn't even given a lecture! Like a prisoner at the gallows getting the governor's pardon, Bill was a free man.

My attention went back to the window, where I could see Barney getting the full brunt of the manager's wrath. "If you can't handle a simple problem like this," — his fingers pointing at Barney's nose – "don't expect me to bail you out." The manager's arms, now raised above his head, had Barney back-peddling. Eventually he got out of the office red-faced, a bead of sweat on his brow, and his once-proud peacock feathers now looked more like a tail between his legs.

Did Barney or Bill learn from this? I couldn't tell you. Did I learn from this? You better believe it. It's much better to bring solutions to your boss rather than problems. If all you bring is problems, it won't take long for them figure out what or who is the real problem. To think people say there's nothing educational on TV! Perhaps they're not watching the right channel.

We're Oookaaay

Every store had its special mix of employees. That mix determined just what kind of personality your store had: very friendly, not-so-friendly, hard working, not-so-hard working, party store, or not-so-much-of-a-party store. The store manager was key in creating the store's personality. The first store manager I worked for was very aware of this and very determined as to what type of store he wanted. Mr. Leschuk wanted a hard-working party store, so we worked hard so we could party. I always believed Mr. Leschuk saw this as a way to reinforce positive behaviour.

Every store had part-time staff with a cocky attitude, thinking the store couldn't survive without them. They often thought they could do better than the full-time staff, but they'd never had ownership of a department. They would usually help clean up an area that needed extra attention and then take credit for fixing it.

Our store had such a group: Brent (best frozen food clerk I ever saw), Scott (fastest box cutter this side of the Rockies), Bill (had the ability to get things done, but to this day it still baffles me as to how he did it!), and Dave (that's me). We worked hard and partied even harder. We were also all in university. So when the opportunity to party presented itself, we always gave that infamous one hundred ten percent. I personally think we started the concept of the now highly successful videos 'Girls Gone Wild.' Unfortunately for us, the world wasn't ready for 'Grocery Clerks Gone Wild.'

It was reading week (spring break) at the university, and the four of us decided we would go out to Bill's family's cabin in B.C. In those days, the store wasn't open on Sunday. The plan was to leave right after work Saturday night. It's about a four-hour drive from Calgary through the Crowsnest Pass on a fairly good road, but it was night and still winter. The four of us thought it best to drive together.

We left the store with all the essentials packed for a successful weekend: beer, rye, steaks, and more beer.

I was driving and, in the spirit of safety, thought it was wise not to risk fatigue when travelling with so many important people.

Safety first! I carefully plotted several rest stops along the way: Fort Macleod (tavern), Pincher Creek (party at the Cow Palace), Sparwood (tavern), the Prince Hotel (tavern), and finally the Jaffery Inn (tavern).

We were very lucky on that trip. Our actions weren't very responsible, but we learn as we grow. We managed to get to Bill's cabin in an impressive seven hours. We could have done it in six and a half if it hadn't been for a small bladder problem that seemed to plague us all.

It was now 2:00 am and we were reflecting on the antics of the trip: the group of local Pincher Creek boys concerned that we leave their town safely and quickly as they chased us out of the party; the local RCMP detachment outside the party that ensured we did; the deer on the road that just missed being featured as the special of the day at the ABC restaurant in Fernie; that ever-so-brief moment on that small patch of black ice. I can still remember the guys screaming like little girls.

It suddenly hit me that Mr. Leschuk must be worried sick about us. Without us, the store might just possibly have to shut its doors permanently – not to mention his concern for his own personal job security. After all, major corporations do not let senior officials fly together for fear of possible tragedies. He was also the father figure in the store and this was like a business trip. The only decent thing to do was to call John and let him know we were safe.

To this day I still remember his phone number. The phone rang three times before I heard a groggy voice answer, "Eh hem," followed by "Hellooo," in a very faint, not-quite-awake voice.

"John! It's us! We're at the lake and we're oookaaay! You can go to bed now!" With a very slight chuckle, Mr. Leschuk was able to squeeze out, "Oh. That's fine boys...thanks for calling."

What a bunch of fine, caring, responsible, young adults we are. Job well done. We quickly toasted our leader, and then continued on with the rest of the weekend.

Five years later, I was at another store. I hadn't seen Brent and Scott in at least four years. Bill was married and living out of town. I was dating a girl who very often would phone me late at night with a crisis. I got very good at answering the phone on one ring.

Some items in this picture may have been
altered to protect the guilty

This particular night the phone rang at 3:00 am. I fumbled the phone but got it on the first ring. "Hello," I said, clearing my throat at the same time. "Dave! John Leschuk here! I'm in Winnipeg and I'm oookaaay!"

With a very slight chuckle I was able to squeeze out, "Oh, that's fine John...thanks for calling." As I hung up the phone, I heard a roar of laughter on the other end. I thought to myself, payback is oookaaay!

A Penny for Your Thoughts

It was a Thursday night. Bill, Scott, and I were in the backroom cutting and marking the next week's specials. For the part-time clerks, this job was like sanctuary. It would take most of the night, and if we played our cards right, we wouldn't have to be on the sales floor or up front to wrap groceries the entire evening. As hard as we worked in the back, it was nothing compared to dealing with customers. Believe it or not, the customers always were and always will be the most work. I still needed to mature a bit more before a true appreciation of dealing with people fully developed.

Our goal to be invisible did not coincide with Jerry, our assistant manager-in-training, who had a completely different plan. He wanted to send us to whichever part of the store we were needed. He had the right idea, just the wrong people. Jerry called us up front. We decided we would stay at the back and finish our job. After all, we thought it better to finish one job before we started another.

After about five minutes, Jerry located us exactly where he had left us. Somewhat agitated, he asked us why we weren't up front wrapping groceries. One of us replied "Jerry, we thought you wanted us to finish this first." As weak as this response was, Jerry's response would soon come back to bite him on the ass.

"You thought. You thought. You're not paid to think. You're paid to do as you're told!"

With that explanation of our job description, the three of us went up front. Later that evening we were able to continue our task of pricing the next week's specials. Just before our coffee break, we noticed Jerry going into the compressor room, which consisted of ten motors used to generate the power to maintain all the freezer and refrigeration units in the store. It was very loud and extremely hot – not a very pleasant place to be. It was now time for our coffee break and we wanted to get the skid we were working on out of the way. Without thinking, we parked the skid in front of the compressor room doors.

This coffee break wasn't as pleasant as we were accustomed. Our usually peaceful rest period was continually disrupted by a loud banging on the compressor room doors and these annoying ear-piercing screams, "Let me out! Let me out!" The magnitude of these screams increased for the duration of our break. We soon returned to our work area. As we cleared the skid from the doors, Jerry immediately came crashing through. He looked liked he had just ran a marathon. His face was ghostly white, his usually crisp white shirt was totally drenched in sweat, and he was breathing heavy. He was trying to control his rage at the same time we were trying to turn our smugness into sincere concern.

Jerry demanded to know why we had placed the skid in front of the doors. I explained in a very convincing tone, "We wanted to get the skid out of the way. We didn't think anybody was in the compressor room. But that's right, we're not paid to think, are we?" Not another word was ever mentioned about the events of that evening.

Just a Closer Walk With Thee

My journey through the grocery industry wasn't a direct path from start to finish. I was a man who learned many trades. I babysat and was willing to change diapers for fifty cents an hour. This was a great initiation for the assistant utility clerk assignment I had a few years later. I was also a paperboy for *The Vancouver Sun*. This job gave me an appreciation for Mondays, the day that traditionally was the thinnest paper, making it the easiest to deliver. The only other job I had was when I was twenty. A lot of kids of that age need to find themselves, usually lost somewhere in Europe or Australia. I didn't realize I was lost until the dean of the University of Calgary suggested that my marks indicated I was very lost. So where did this good old Canadian boy go to find himself? The West Coast of Vancouver Island, to become a logger!

This job was great and there are many entertaining stories about my adventures. However, this is not one of them. This story is about my grandma. On the weekends I was out of camp, she let me stay with her in North Vancouver. I was born there and had a good friend Jim, who still lived there. It was actually Jim's dad that helped me get the logging job. Now my grandma (on my mom's side) was very special. She always had a mischievous sparkle in her eyes that, combined with her smile, made her face just simply light up. No matter how old she was, you could always see the child inside her. Grandma was full of surprises.

One Saturday night, my Uncle Walter (her brother) was over for dinner. Jim came over and we were going to the pub. Grandma thought it was best that Jim have a quick drink before we go. After all, he was a favourite of both Grandma's and Uncle Walter's. My grandma had this habit of tilting her glass while holding it. The scotch would touch the inside rim of the glass, but amazingly never once did the scotch touch the outside of the rim. Never a drop was spilled.

Well, a bottle of Drambuie and half a bottle of Passport scotch later, Jim and I were treated to a complete re-enactment of the 1927 Greater Vancouver Open Charleston Dance Competition. This event was won by a brother and sister team – my grandma and Uncle Walter. They regained the title again that night.

The last weekend I stayed over, Grandma asked if I could do her a favour. She explained that her other brother Robert was in the closet. Now this was a surprise to me. Robert had been crippled by arthritis very early in life. For a moment I wasn't sure if Grandma was outing her brother or not. I reminded Grandma he had been dead for fifteen years. She still insisted Uncle Robert was in the closet. For just a moment Norman Bates flashed in my thoughts. Grandma went to the closet and pulled down a box from the top shelf. My Uncle Robert's ashes were inside. There was momentary relief until I realized there was a dead person in the box.

The plan was to spread Robert's ashes off of Point Atkinson in West Vancouver, a very beautiful place. Grandma needed me to give her a ride. I had a 1965 Mustang fastback that I loved. As foolish as it sounds, I wasn't comfortable driving with a box of human remains. However, it was the right thing to do so I did it.

It was a typical Vancouver weekend, overcast with an annoying drizzle that just wouldn't stop. You know the type: wipers on, wipers off, repeat. Ford had not equipped the early Mustangs with time delay wipers. Grandma was dressed for the rain. She wore one of those clear plastic kerchiefs to protect her hair, a raincoat, and Uncle Robert tucked securely under her arm.

Jim Rackham

My 1965 Mustang/Hearse

So off we go to West Vancouver in my poppy red Mustang/hearse. I drove as quickly as possible to Light House Park. The cliffs overlooking Burrard Inlet where Uncle Robert was to finally rest are located in this park.

The half-mile path to the shore was wet and very slippery. I held my grandma under my arm and she held her brother under hers. We all made it safely to the point. It really was a beautiful and dramatic scene. The waves crashing in on the rocky shore sent white, foaming water into the gray sky. The wind was blowing the rain hard enough to sting my face and make it difficult to see. My grandma asked to have a minute alone with her brother. With the wind and the rain, I was concerned that she might slip on the rocks. I only took a couple of steps back, just in case.

I wasn't the best outdoorsman, but there are a couple of things I know you don't stand down wind from: a chicken farm or a brush fire. I very quickly found a third. As my grandma started shaking Uncle Robert's remains into the ocean, they were met with a gusting offshore wind. Most of my uncle blew behind Grandma, right into me.

I'm not proud of my actions that followed. I was only grateful that my grandma didn't see me; she was staring into the sea where she believed her brother to be. Anybody else would have thought I was being attacked by a swarm of killer bees, arms swinging, my head bobbing and weaving, running away from that cloud of ash. Grandma just turned and started walking back to the car. There was a calmness about her. Her brother, who lived through most of his life in pain, was finally at peace.

Once in a while a family member will say to me, "I can see a little of your Uncle Robert in you." I think it will remain a mystery to them why I always politely excuse myself and go wash my face and clean my ears.

Putting On the Shine

It was the late seventies and I was still part-time at Safeway. However, in the summers while university was out I was available to work full-time. This particular summer I was assigned the envious position of assistant utility clerk. My grandpa would have used the term 'porter.' The actual job was janitor. Now I realize the job sounds pretty impressive, but remember, I was only the assistant to the number one utility clerk.

My day always started with the employees' washrooms. Cleaning, sanitizing, and polishing three sinks, three toilets, and two urinals. Included, but not limited to, were the cubicle walls and doors, the washroom walls and doors, and, of course, the floors. I was also the go-to guy responsible for keeping things moving in there. I wasn't one to be afraid to take the plunge, or plunger. I would be remiss if I didn't take this opportunity to speak on behalf of all the commercial washroom sanitation engineers: Ladies, please use the receptacle provided. Those things just aren't meant for flushing!

Now the glory job of this position wasn't the washrooms. I know that's hard to believe. The job that put the assistant utility clerk's position into a similar category as fireman, airline pilot, and professional sports figure was the once-a-week waxing of the floors.

The wet look lives!

There are very few jobs with such instant gratification than turning a dirty, shop-worn floor into a brilliantly glistening floor with what we in the industry call the 'wet look.' Two indicators were used to measure a successful wax and buff: first, people would stop to touch it because it still looked wet. Second, women wearing skirts would move quickly and carefully, aware that standing still could prove embarrassing, as the mirror-like reflection from the floor could allow for some very candid observations.

During my time as the assistant utility clerk, I was fortunate to work with the first utility clerk, Alex. Alex was all of five foot three, with slivery thinning hair, thick Buddy Holly-style glasses, and still very fit for his sixty-five years. This gentleman epitomized the phrase 'work smarter not harder.' He also took a lot of pride in 'the shine.' After each wax I would find an out of the way place on the floor to write with my finger in the semi-wet wax, "Floors by Alex and Dave." I gave Alex top billing out of respect. When the sun hit that part of the floor, the message lit up like neon. Yes, I was proud of the job we did.

Harry was assistant manager at the time. He possessed similar qualities of Felix Unger from *The Odd Couple*; very neurotic when it came to cleaning and everything had to have its place. He once had a carpenter put shelves over our utility sink in the back room. This would have been great except for Harry's rule: absolutely nothing was to go on these shelves! He was also colour blind. Harry's wife would pick out his clothes each morning. Remember, this was the seventies and clothes were very colourful. Once in a while Harry would come to work in purple pants, an olive green shirt, a multi-coloured tie, and a black and white checked sports coat. Did I mention the matching white belt and white shoes? Usually Alex would say something like, "Fighting with the wife, Harry?" "Ya, how'd you know?" would be Harry's puzzled response, and Alex would just counter with "Wild guess."

This one particular morning, the rising sun was dancing across our freshly waxed floors like a magnificent ballet. Alex and I took a moment to absorb the spiritual experience. I had to get Harry to admit these floors looked great.

You see, getting a compliment from Harry came as frequently as Haley's Comet, about once every seventy-six years. I walked up to Harry as proud as any seventeen year old could be about the shine of a floor. "Harry, are these not the best floors you've ever seen?" I boasted.

He slid his glasses down his nose so we were looking eye to eye. "Not even close." Harry explained everything he felt was wrong. I looked over to Alex, who was shaking his head. Not at Harry's comments but at my failed attempt at getting praise.

I dragged my shattered ego over to Alex. "David (he always called me David when he wanted to make a point), if you are happy with the floors you don't need Harry's seal of approval. But if you feel it necessary, watch me."

Alex walked up to Harry with a surrendering pose. "Harry," he said, "I want to apologize for the mess these floors are in. I'm not happy with them. I promise we'll do better." Harry, with disbelief on his face, put his arm around Alex and said, "Are you kidding? These floors are great!" Harry continued with the accolades while Alex looked over my way and gave me a 'stick with me, kid' kind of wink. The floors weren't the only things Alex could put a shine on.

It's Magenta

There was always a healthy rivalry between stores. This went beyond who had the nicest store or the largest volume. It frequently included games of athletic competitions, after which a party almost certainly followed and the competition would continue. Egos, liquor, pride, youth, and members of the opposite sex made for some very exciting events. Our store was one of the largest in the city and we had a group of employees that could outperform most others in just about anything inside the store or out.

We played tackle football with a neighbouring store on a Sunday. These games were played without equipment and became very physical and extremely punishing. It was not unusual to make a trip to the emergency ward after the game. This particular game was a one-sided affair that left the other team badly beaten and their quarterback's ego totally crushed. Randy was about six foot four and weighed about one hundred seventy pounds. The best way to describe him would be tall and gangly. He had not quite grown into his body or mind yet. After the severe beating, 58-0, Randy was somewhat less than a good sport. Of course, we probably weren't the most gracious winners. Some cutting remarks followed by a lot of laughter may have helped feed Randy's temper.

It's funny how time affects different aspects of life. It was about three years later and my cousin Bruce and I went to a house party. It seemed that every weekend someone from the store would host a party. We entered the house and it was full of festive people, loud music, and lots of liquor. I scanned the party for familiar faces and for faces with which I would like to become familiar. I noticed one face that stood above the crowd. Randy was still six foot four, but time had filled him out. He was now about two hundred fifty pounds. When he spotted us, he immediately plowed through the crowd to greet us. He directed his attention to my cousin. Randy looked at Bruce's Lacoste shirt, and asked, "Is that a pink shirt? Only faggots wear pink shirts." Bruce, in his best Liberace impression answered, "It's not pink; it's magenta."

As tall as Randy was, great comebacks still flew over his head. Time did wonders filling out his body but still left his head vacant. Randy was obviously looking to start something, or finish something, probably the game.

I saw a chance to get out of this conversation and I headed to the kitchen. I was talking to some people near the beer when Randy came in for round two. "So Rackham, where are you working now?" I answered, "Still at Safeway," and Randy came up with another shot: "Only losers work at Safeway." So I asked Randy what he was doing. He replied, "Playing football at Simon Fraser University." You know when you have a chance to make that perfect comeback, but drop the ball instead? This was not one of those times. "Randy, I've seen you play football; I sure hope you're studying hard!" Well, this might not had been the best time to have such a brilliant comeback. He pushed me, but it would take more than that to provoke me into a fight with a university ball player. The second push got a response from Randy's girlfriend. "Randy, not again. Please don't fight him." This was not what I wanted to hear. The third push created that stop-the-music situation when everybody ends his or her conversation and looks to see what will happen next. I'm not a fighter, but this seemed like one of those times you just had to stand up for yourself. I said, "We'll dance, but not in the house," and turned to towards the door. This was to give enough time for someone, anyone, to talk Randy out of this potential conflict. As I was opening the door and saw Bruce, I indicated I was going outside and he may want to watch. Bruce was quick and realized it was time to get reinforcements (my buddy Bill). It was raining outside, one more reason not to fight. I felt a pair of very large hands on my shoulders, not pulling me back but pushing me forward, down the stairs. Luckily I caught myself, but now I was angry.

I was on the sidewalk floating like a butterfly and ready to sting like a bee. While I was dancing, Randy was swinging. His knuckles just nicked the tip of my nose. It then hit me that I was actually in a fight. I was hoping that's all that would hit me.

Driven by panic and fear, I got the SFU football player in a headlock and started to throw a flurry of as many punches as I possibly could. I'm certain that one of the two punches I threw landed just before he picked me up and threw me into the ditch. My brand new sweater was now soaking up the ditch water. As I was on my back in the ditch thinking this is not good, I noticed the undercarriage of a 1978 Honda Civic. Never had much appreciation for that car, but this would soon change.

Randy was on top of me drawing back his hammer-like fist. All I could think about was that after this was over, my nose may be so far on the other side of my face, I'd most likely smell ear wax for months. I was partially under the beautiful Civic and trying to squirm even deeper into the bowels of the car. Whatever works as sanctuary is okay with me! As Randy prepared to release his barrage of punches, I was able to grab his collar and introduce his head to the Honda's bumper. Now as I said before, time had not filled his head with anything that might resemble brain waves. He pulled his fist back again, I pulled his collar again, and again he met the best Japanese import ever! At this point I heard Bill's voice say, "We should break this up." I was in total agreement! I felt Randy had had enough. It was the next comment from a co-worker that I will remember for a very long time. "Nah, let them go at it a bit longer." Easy to say for someone standing in an upright position and minus two hundred fifty pounds. on their chest! Thank God cooler heads prevailed and the six or so onlookers dragged this slightly miffed linebacker off of me.

Bill was holding me up and pulling me towards him, making it look like I was still interested in continuing the main event. I was back-pedaling faster than Prime Minister Pierre Trudeau during the "fuddle duddle" incident. Bill looked at me with alarm, stating, "You're cut, there's blood all over you." I was a little worried but more relieved as I felt no pain. A cut heals, but pain could leave an embarrassing scar on my ego. I'm a wimp when it comes to pain. If I was seen crying like a baby I wouldn't have been able to live that down. Bill took a closer look and then realized that the blood wasn't mine!

We turned to look at my opponent and noticed blood gushing from his nose and even better, his pants were split from the crotch, heading south then abruptly turning north all the way back up to his belt.

Now a lot of people would have hung around for the accolades of such a brilliant display of pugilism. I, however, over the years have had lots of growth between my ears. I knew when the getting was good. Randy, I am told, sat on the hood of that Civic for three hours before he finally went to the emergency ward. I, fortunately, have not run into Randy since that night. If I had I am certain this would have been the last of my short stories.

A White Sports Coat

It was the early eighties and I had been full-time for about two years, and the third man in the store for about six months. I had turned a part-time job into a career and was being transferred to a new assignment: to join the re-line crew. This new job was a jumping off point, hopefully to an assistant manager's position. I was experiencing mixed emotions about moving. I was safe in this store. All my friends and what I thought to be potential girlfriends were in this store. I wasn't sure if I enjoyed the job, or if it was the camaraderie of the people. I knew the next few months would be the telltale.

Barrie Onofrychuk

The re-line crew; responsible for positioning 35,000 items into the store. However ask us to do a jigsaw puzzle, no way.

With me leaving the store, it made room for another 'up and comer' to take my spot. I've mentioned that the third man position was an assignment that the company would use to determine the potential leadership qualities of a particular individual. It was very important that this person had the respect of the other clerks. Brian, a very enthusiastic and hard working clerk, was going to take my vacated job. If he had a weakness it might be that he lacked the ability to think on his feet. Brian was a great planner, but in our business you must be able to make quality decisions on the spot. A moment's hesitation could have serious implications.

Our industry is also made up of many traditions. These sacred practices have been handed down from journeyman clerks to newly hired clerks over many years, similar to how the elders of ancient tribes passed on the old ways to their young warriors.

One of the most sacred of all the grocery traditions is the baptizing of the young clerks as they start their journey into the world outside of the store. This ceremony is a coming of age for the clerk. To put it another way, if you leave the store, the produce sink (equivalent to a bathtub) gets filled up with ice and water, and one way or another the clerk leaving is going for a swim.

There are three options for the clerk designated for the dunking: go peacefully and no one gets hurt, fight like a madman hanging on to the slim hope you'll get away, or my personal favourite, take as many down with you as you can.

Make no mistake, one way or another you're going in -- my thinking was to make as many people pay the price with you. You're still wet but you feel a whole lot better when you're not the only one!

My last day at the store was a Saturday. As happy as I was for the move, Brian was even happier. He came into work wearing a very sharp-looking white sports coat. This new coat symbolized Brian's new position of power. After a brief fashion show, the coat was very carefully hung up in the back office.

Having experienced this baptizing ritual before, from the other side, gave me a slight advantage: the element of surprise was removed. As was tradition, Brian took the role as the leader. I didn't give the enviable swim much thought until about five o'clock. That was when I heard Brian calling all the clerks to the front of the store to share his plan and recruit his followers.

I was in the back office, basically cornered, but I was ready. I had come to accept the fact I was going in the sink. I continued to do my paperwork in the office as if I knew nothing of the upcoming initiation. Moments later, Brian called to me from outside the office door.

He had recruited eight other clerks to assist in the baptism. I was sitting with my back to the now very excited group of parishioners. I spun my chair around, stood up, and faced the mob. Brian was positioned in front of his followers. His face, turning from confidently in control with a grin wider than an aisle, to a look of sheer horror and helplessness. I stood with a can of aerosol whipping cream in each of my hands, and wearing a very sharp white sports coat. Animals are always most dangerous when cornered.

Someone in the mob screamed, "Let's get him!" Brian turned to his followers and said, "Hold it! He's got my new sports coat on!" Everyone stopped for a moment and looked at each other in confusion. Jack, the clerk who would fill Brian's vacated position, looked at every one and said, "It's not my coat, let's get him!" Well, what happened next was not for the faint of heart or for lovers of fine haberdasheries. Water, whipping cream, and wet polyester were everywhere. I went in the sink all right, but not without dampening the spirits of a few others.

It's funny, Brian eventually left the company and Jack is now a store manager. This industry is not rocket science, but you do need the ability to think on your feet.

Would You Like the Rim Salted?

The grocery business is based on a very simple principle. We have stuff, the customer has money; they trade us their money for our stuff. It was always believed the more stuff we have the more money the customer will trade. That belief created one of the greatest love-hate relationships the industry has ever known: the roller coaster relationship between the corporate buyers and the retail stores. Similar to the relationship a sports fan has with a referee. Make a good call and you're okay in their book; make a bad call and you're a bum! Now that I think about it, the best a referee could do in my mind was be okay and I don't ever recall giving a buyer better than an okay. For the sake of accuracy, we better change that to "The greatest okay-hate relationships."

The buyers would very often fill your store with items they believed would sell. The retailers always knew what would sell but were wise enough to keep our comments to ourselves, or at least wait a few weeks and measure the amount of dust on a product to determine the sales success. This method had a very high accuracy rating.

It was the early eighties and we had a new product distributed to us that the buyers thought would sell extremely well: Motts Clamato Juice. We were sent three hundred cases of tomato juice mixed with the juice of a clam? What was the buyer thinking, or better yet smoking? I predicted this to be a dud. We would be better off trying to sell rocks as pets! I made two other predictions that year: Wayne Gretzky won't make it in the NHL, and the Internet would be a passing fad. Apparently, not my best year for predictions.

It was Saturday at about five o'clock. The store manager called me to the back room; as third man I was responsible for the condition of the back room area. Clean, organized and as little stock as possible. The manager was standing by a skid of the clamato juice. I knew he was going to ask about it. I thought to myself, we didn't order it; it's displayed on the front end, in the lobby, on a table in the back aisle, and a floor stack in front of the shelf. It's not my fault!

However, I was always taught to take responsibility for my actions and my area without making a lot of excuses. Sure enough the, manager looked at me and asked, "What is this?" his hand on a case of the 'red nectar.' I carefully thought out my reply. "We didn't order it; it's displayed on the front end, in the lobby, on a table in the back aisle, and a floor stack in front of the shelf. It's not my fault!" I was always a better coach than a player. I looked at my boss, my leader, and said, "I don't know what else to do."

I always said our profession is not rocket science, but you must know how to think on your feet. My manager looked disappointed that I couldn't have thought of another way to reduce the amount of clamato in the store. The look changed to a very pleased expression as he was about to inform me of his plan to reduce inventory. My manager slid his hand into his pocket and pulled out a ten-dollar bill. As he handed it to me, he instructed me to, "Go get a bottle of vodka." Now that's thinking outside of the box and into the bottle. After three trips to the liquor store, we put a dent in the remaining inventory.

This ended up being a joint effort with the meat and produce departments helping out. It wasn't a pretty sight in the back room after we finished reducing the excess inventory. I was asked to come in Sunday and clean up the mess. If the price for the lessons learned was only cleaning up the back room, it was a bargain. I learned there's always another way, and Caesars are a very good drink. clamato juice just might become a top seller. Who knows maybe Gretzky can make an impression in the NHL and just maybe this Internet thing will stick around. Being a good Calgarian, I finally settled on the Internet, maybe, Gretzky no way. Still, two out of three isn't bad.

Classic Caesar Recipe

- 4 ounces clam tomato juice

- 1 ounces vodka

- celery stalk

- 2 teaspoons lime juice

- salt & pepper to taste

- 1 dash Tabasco® hot pepper sauce

- 2 dashes Worcestershire® sauce

* If you choose to drink, please choose to drink responsibly.

Hitchin' a Ride

Life lessons can be learned from many different experiences. The key is recognizing the opportunities when they come. This is the story of my first week logging and 'pilgrimage' from camp (Rankin Cove in the Tofino Inlet) to North Vancouver. A huge opportunity. I had successfully survived my first week logging, by the narrowest of margins; I believe a photo finish was required! I was in a world so different from what I was used to, leaving level ground and sunshine and exchanging it for hills and rain. Those two combinations added up to me falling more than the trees we cut. I needed a little sanctuary and I was in my Mustang heading for the safe haven of North Vancouver. I had many friends and relatives there and was looking forward to a relaxing weekend sharing my stories of my first week at the new job.

The 1965 Mustang fastback is a timeless car, but after fifteen years, time had made it less than dependable. I was halfway between Ucuelet and Port Alberni when my car lost a long but valiantly fought battle with its thermostat. The highway I was on would best be described as desolate, dark, and dangerous. It was just an old logging road with some asphalt thrown over top. This wasn't a road you hitch-hiked on; this was a road you flagged a car down on. I was standing in the middle of the road for about ten minutes and thankfully, the only car that came by, stopped to see how they could help. Island people are very friendly, and this gentleman had no problem offering me a ride into Port Alberni, along with a pull on his half-full bottle of Canadian Club wrapped in the conventional brown paper bag.

It was a very exciting ride into Port with this highly spirited sports fan. My driver informed me he was on his way to Nanaimo for an evening of "All-Star Wrestling." I was not that confident either of us was going to make our destinations. Most of the wrestling was done with the steering wheel, trying to negotiate the extremely sharp corners and stay on the road. Now that I think about it, the straight-a-ways also provided a challenge.

We eventually made it into Port Alberni, with the help of some prayers on my part. As we entered the town I spotted a service station and a hotel. I got my newfound friend to drop me off, gave him a twenty, and thanked him for the ride. I got the service station to go get my car and they said they would work on it Saturday. All that was left was to check into the Arlington Hotel. The old saying, "Don't judge a book by its cover" can be used similarly with hotels, "Don't judge a hotel by its sign." The Arlington Hotel had a nice sign.

I entered what I thought was the lobby. There was a sign that said lobby, but I ended up in the tavern. Usually not a bad thing, but I was tired and just wanted a clean, comfortable bed. I figured I must have missed a door somewhere so I tried again. Again I ended up in the tavern. I recognized one of the fallers from camp sitting at the bar and asked him where the lobby was. "You're in it," he said. "If you want a room you get it from the bartender." Now I've stayed in motels where the gas bar attendant booked you into the room, so this wasn't so different. I got the bartender's attention and asked him for a room. He in turn asked, "How long do you need it?" I answered, "Just one night." He looked at me as if I was from another planet. "The whole night? Kid, you must be lost. Tell me your story!"

I told him and he informed me of a bus leaving for Nanaimo at 10:15: it was now 10:00 pm. The bartender added that the ferry leaves Nanaimo for Vancouver at midnight. All right, with any luck, I could still make it to North Van in time for breakfast.

I caught the bus with minutes to spare but was faced with yet another decision. Including the bus driver, there were just three of us on this Scenicruiser. The other passenger chose to sit in the middle of the bus, most likely suffering from a fear of commitment. I had three choices: I could sit at the back of the bus by myself, I could sit with the other traveller, or I could sit up front with the bus driver. I figured I would sit up front with the driver. Considering my most recent experience, I thought it best to keep an eye on him. The view from the bus while passing other cars was very educational. I had a great vantage point, looking down into the cars driving along side of the bus.

It seemed that drinking from a brown paper bag while driving wasn't restricted to just wrestling fans. Maybe it was just a popular way to pass the time on a Friday night.

It was easy to identify me as a logger. I had my gear with me and I was still wearing some of it, as I had no time to change. Paul Bunyan I wasn't, but I could possibly be mistaken for his lesser known brother, Peter Bunyan. If you were a logger on the Island you were treated like a celebrity. People just couldn't do enough for you. I was talking to the bus driver, one of the few drivers that night not pulling from a brown paper bag, and sharing my perils of the day. The other passenger got off in Coombs, the very next town. The driver informed me that the bus doesn't arrive in Nanaimo until 12:15 am, and the bus depot is on the other side of town from the ferry terminal. I must have had that lost puppy dog face because the driver looked at me and said, "Aw hell, I'll get you there and in time." With that, the driver put the pedal to the floor and I sank deep into my seat as the bus accelerated. If only my Mustang could perform like this; we were flying down the highway! I took a quick moment to check under the driver's seat, just to see if there was a brown paper bag I might have missed.

We drove right by the bus depot, on some very narrow streets, made some corners I didn't think possible, and ended up at the ferry terminal at 11:55 pm. This bus driver could have put race car driver Mario Andretti to shame. I thanked him, collected my gear, thanked him again, and then ran to the gate. As the bus was driving away, I heard a couple of blasts on the horn in farewell.

A man, his bus, and a mission equals one unforgettable ride.

Now life has its peaks and valleys. To live right, you better get used to handling these fluctuations. The more you experience life, the better you handle the sudden changes in elevation. This trip had many of them, with one more still to come. As I got to the gate, I noticed a heavy chain and lock on it. A sign read "Ferry in Dry Dock until February 2." It was January 10!

Mother's Day

It was a Saturday morning at the store, shortly before our 8:00 am opening. There was serenity in the store, usually created by the absence of customers. This is when the store looked it best. The night crew has the shelves full and faced. The floor crew has worked their magic and put a shine to the tiles that only hours ago you'd have thought impossible. The bakery's heavenly odour of fresh bread wafts across the store. The produce is crisp and full. Nothing to worry about; the store is ready for another day of sales. All that's required are customers spending money and to serve them.

The half hour before the store opens can also be an emotionally perplexing time. You can admire the hard work of your staff and at the same time dread the inevitable phone calls from employees who can't make it in to work. A mysterious plague tends to sweep through all grocery stores on the weekends. I often compared it to the Black Death that plagued Europe during the Middle Ages. If you are sick, you are to contact the store as quickly as possible, allowing time to replace the shift.

This particular morning the phone rang just before the opening of the doors. Our head teller (person who was responsible for the front end, the cashiers, and courtesy clerks) answered the phone as usual. "Good morning, Louise speaking, how can I help you?" A female voice on the other end replied, "Good morning, this is Doug's mother calling. Doug is very sick and won't be able to work today." Louise replied, "That's too bad, I hope he gets better soon." Doug's mother said, "He should be well enough to work tomorrow, but I am keeping him in bed for today." Louise said, "That's great, just one thing…we have three Dougs in this store, Doug who?" The other end was silent. "Hello," Louise said. Doug's mother replied, "Just a minute." Louise could hear the mother asking, "What's your last name?" A moment later the last name was offered.

There's an old saying in our industry. Prior planning prevents poor performances. Unfortunately, I must not have communicated this to Doug. He showed up to work on the Sunday. I looked at Doug; he sheepishly returned the look. "Three days, Doug," referring to the length of his suspension. Doug, looking embarrassed, simply said, "Sounds fair."

Not Too Tough To Change

I've worked with many different people in my career, but I've found that for the most part they all have one thing in common.

I remember taking a boat across the Tofino Inlet going into the logging camp for the first time. The camp was a beautiful site nestled in a small cove with the mountains cascading into the very dark and deep water. It was dusk, so the light was turning that dreary, depressing gray and the weather was doing what it does best in the coastal rain forest: raining. It was a very lonely feeling in this isolated place, yet it was very peaceful and serene too.

It didn't take long before these impressions suddenly changed. As the boat was pulling up to the wharf, I noticed a very nervous man standing on the dock with his suitcase and two very intimidating gentlemen standing beside him. I suspected that this was not the Welcome Wagon committee waiting to introduce me to the camp. As the boat was pulling up, one of the 'gentlemen' picked up the suitcase and heaved it into the still-moving boat. The very nervous gentleman quickly followed the suitcase into the boat with a little help from his friends. "If you ever come in this camp calling yourself a cook again, it won't be a boat we'll be tossing you in." This comment came from the thrower of the suitcase.

I got onto the wharf trying to act casual, but also avoiding any and all eye contact. I didn't need to upset anyone my first minute. As the boat pulled away, the now not-so- nervous cook decided it was safe to share a few choice words of his own. The further the boat got away from the dock, the more colourful the expressions. I learned quickly that the cook was the most important position in a logging camp. If you weren't very good, you weren't around very long.

These were the guys I was going to live with every day of the week; work with them, eat with them, play with them, and share the old ATCO trailer with them. (Note to self, check the lock on your room door.) Getting to know these guys was a slow process.

They were a little cool to outsiders, and being a green one from Alberta didn't help the situation. I can remember one of the fallers saying, "If another farmer from Alberta comes out here to log, I think I'll go to Alberta to farm."

These were tough men. I think most had spent some time in jail, and the others hadn't been caught yet. The six months I was in camp, we had several broken bones, one severed finger (it was found two weeks later and tossed around the cookhouse), one broken back, and one death. If two guys had a beef with each other, it was settled with fisticuffs, Friday after work, at the dock on the other side of the inlet. Of course, it wasn't without some sort of etiquette; as the winner always bought the loser a beer afterwards.

My daily routine was to get up at 6:00 am, go to the cookhouse; I'd have breakfast, get my gear on, and be in the marshalling yard by 7:30. This is where we would catch the crummy (bus) to our work site. I was never sure why they called the bus a crummy; the only thing I could think of was it described the ride. After work, I'd be back at the camp by 5:15 pm, shower, get dinner by 6:00, then head over to the recreation trailer to shoot a game of pool, get a pack of Life Savers, watch TV until 9:00, and then check my lock and go to bed.

I am certain these crummies (busses) helped to inspire teleworking!

It was very regimented. Seldom did anyone wander from this simplest of lifestyles. After about one month, I decided to get brave and suggested a TV show to watch. I wasn't sure I had the balls to suggest this show; it didn't fit the image. It was artsy, witty, and very humourous. The characters were deep, unique, and very likable. It had nothing in common with loggers. What the heck, I took a chance. "Hey, how about we watch The Muppet Show?" "The fuckin' what show?" was the response of the other guys. They all had a look on their faces as if they were sucking lemons. I knew exactly what they were thinking. Not only is he from Alberta, but he likes to play with dolls (note to self, check lock on room door).

A few weeks went by and every Wednesday at 7:30, I tried to enlighten this group of tobacco chewing, bar brawling, and Muppet mauling individuals, all to no avail. Until one day a special guest on the show was influential enough to get this group of homophobic loggers to watch puppets on TV. Raquel Welch had the magic to get the still-reluctant bunch to at least sit down and watch the show. After this episode, the camp ritual changed, at least on Wednesday nights. Dinner, Life Savers, a quick game of pool, then grab your seat 'cause the TV room was standing room only, filled with tough guys watching the Muppets and howling with laughter, regardless of the guest stars.

It was tough trying to create change. It also required courage for these men to enjoy a show that in the past they would have made jokes about the people watching it. The one thing that we all have in common - we all love to laugh!

I Got the Beat

In order to better understand our industry and how it was run for many years, you need to go back to World War II. At the end of the war, the grocery industry experienced very rapid growth. The servicemen coming back from overseas found employment in our industry, bringing with them a very militaristic work ethic. As these people got promoted to management so did their military style. Our industry became very disciplined and extremely good at following orders. As we moved into the sixties and seventies this style of management often leads to conflicts with the baby boomers and their 'questioning attitudes.' This lead to some interesting situations, as the transition of power gradually changed hands.

Store managers were required to attend the weekly district meeting. This was a meeting held by the district manager (usually in a boardroom at head office/headquarters). The purpose was to use this time to facilitate a positive two-way communication forum between the district manager, 'The Field General' and the store manager, 'The Platoon Captain.' I believe the idea was to use these meetings to explain strategic battle plans for the future and receive feedback on the success of battle plans currently in use to win the war on sales. However, our district manager (DM) usually bypassed the need for two-way communication. His motto was, listen, understand, and execute.

I was a newly appointed store manager and had all of three months' experience of active duty. Enough experience in my mind to run the war all by myself. After all, it was the eighties, and the computer age contained technical advancements that old soldiers left over from the grocery wars of the past just could not comprehend. Of course the DM saw me as a green soldier with just enough sense to shoot off my mouth and, with a little more effort, shoot myself in the foot. In some cases, this could be deemed as an act of insubordination on the field of battle. In such cases, a swift but fair execution is required.

When attending these meetings, it didn't take long to be initiated to several rituals. One of which was that each manager would sit in the same location every meeting. Heaven forbid you sat in the wrong chair. There was a relationship between the location of your chair that involved the length of service and the size of your store. We were always very aware of the fact that size does matter! The senior managers all sat as far away from the DM as possible, with the most experienced taking his position directly opposite the DM. The green recruits were required to sit on either side of the great general. All within striking distance. Not only did you have to be sharp but also agile!

While at one of these meetings, our DM asked us a question about our practice of doubling the refund if a customer wasn't satisfied with a perishable product. In an unprecedented act of facilitating two way communications, our leader actually asked for our opinion. Then the realization dawned on me: I'd likely be asked for my thoughts first since I sat directly to his right. I must think fast. His attention turned to me. I sorted through the facts, quickly assigned a level of priority to each one, and arrived at the best answer. I confidently explained my logic and unequivocally stated, "Keep the refund offer. We can stand by it!"

There were fifteen managers in that particular meeting, all ready to vote on the future of the policy. There was little discussion after me; I figured I must have explained it very well. So we lifted our hands to yea or nay. The final tally? Keep the policy: one. Get rid of it: fourteen. I now realized how the allied troops must have felt at Dunkirk.

The district manager thought it appropriate to relay a story that his mother had told him. Apparently Momma DM grew up in Europe during World War II. "Every day a troop of soldiers would march by her house in perfect step. All except for one soldier, who was always out of time. Dave, do you get my point?" the DM said to me. Without thinking, I replied, "Or could it be that he was the only soldier in time and all the rest were out of time?" The DM gave me a glare that sent the hairs at the back of my neck standing at attention. At that point I realized I had accomplished two things at once: I had shot my mouth off while shooting myself in the foot.

Passing the Torch

It was February 1988 in Calgary. We were hosting the Olympic Winter Games. This was a magical time for all Calgarians. The entire city was in a euphoric state. People were experiencing a newly found brotherhood with the entire world. We had a civic pride that has never been equalled. All this emotion was gushing out from everyone.

I was managing a small store in the Bowness area of town. Thought to be a tougher part of town but, really it wasn't. Just the stigma left from a couple of bike gangs and the odd murder. I found it to be very community-oriented. Customers didn't expect great service but certainly appreciated it!

It was Saturday and the opening ceremonies for the games were that afternoon. There were to be sixty thousand people at McMahon Stadium to witness all the pageantry of the Olympic experience. At 2:00 pm the torch was to be lit. As the torch was being fired up it was planned that all the churches in Calgary would ring their bells.

Realizing that Tide at $5.99 a box just might not be able to compete with the events of that afternoon, we scheduled our help accordingly. In other words, very thin. At 2:00 pm, I stepped outside. It was cold but I wanted to hear the bells ringing. Right to the second, the bells rang sending goose bumps all over my body. Most likely it was the -15 Celsius temperature that actually generated the bumps, but the bells make for a better story.

At 4:00 pm, the Olympic ceremonies had finished and customers flooded the store. I was at the front wrapping groceries. Both customers and employees loved to see the manager doing that sort of work. I looked up and greeted the next customer. She was an older lady, with wind blown gray hair and so many layers of clothing she looked like the Michelin tire man. This included a very recognizable jacket: the Olympic volunteer jacket. Every one of the eight thousand volunteers got one.

With my uncanny ability to process information, I commented, "I bet you were at the opening ceremonies." This lady looked at me, pushed her shoulders back, and very proudly stated, "I was not! I was at the edge of town and cheered my grandson as he carried the Olympic torch into the city!" Her emotion couldn't be held back and tears began to flow.

I hadn't noticed but the next lady in line was listening to our conversation. She stepped forward and announced, "Well, I was at the opening ceremonies and I watched my granddaughter dance." There were now tears flowing down her face. She was just able to get out, "And she was the best one out there!" These two ladies now stood bawling at the check stand together. They had the attention of many curious onlookers. I knew I should console them. I wanted to console them.

Unfortunately a grocery store can be a very dangerous place. At that exact moment, I must have got some debris or something in my eye. I had to excuse myself; you just don't take chances with your eyesight. A quick flushing of the eye and I was good as new. In this business, you deal with emotions every day. You've got to be careful not to get caught up in the moment, as this may impair your ability to make quality decisions. Thankfully, I never had this problem.

Taco Bell

In 1993, our company experienced some problems with the future. We didn't know if there was going to be one or not. Competitors with lower cost structures had eroded our market share through very competitive pricing. We had to react effectively and quickly. If we couldn't lower our cost structure to keep our prices competitive, well, let's just say this book would be a lot thinner than it is now.

While the company restructured, and offered the employees a buy out, I was offered a job as the director of Retail Support. I would have to report to work in Edmonton, but since the company was restructuring, they didn't want to relocate me right away. Personally, I believed they just wanted to take me for a test drive before buying.

I spent the next eight months living in a hotel in Edmonton. One suitcase and a garment bag. People used to ask me, "How can you stand to live like that, on hotel food, a strange bed, out of a suitcase?" Let me think. All the food that I want, when I want it, and how I want it (paid for with my expense account); a king size bed (an upgrade from my fifteen-year-old queen size bed); my laundry done and my room cleaned every day. My answer was always the same: "You got to do what you got to do." I became very adept at turning the grin on my face into a subtle expression of pain. Not too much, but just enough to let them know the sacrifices I was willing to make for our company.

It was now September, and as all good things must come to an end, so did this ride. In order to save money I was being relocated to the company apartment. It was a nice apartment, two bedrooms, two baths, ten minutes from the office and five to the West Edmonton Mall. The rent was paid for but I became responsible for my meals. Still, all in all a good deal. I moved in on a Friday.

The next Monday, I was at work as usual at 7:00 am. After about an hour, Flo, the DM's admin/assistant, made an announcement over the public address (PA) system that ran throughout the office.

"We have a new member of our Edmonton team joining us today. Jeff has been appointed our new Alberta maintenance manager!" I was thinking, "What is this?"

I didn't get a special announcement when I started here. Flo continued in spite of my dismay. "Jeff is from Winnipeg, and girls… he's cute and single!" Well, this crossed the line! Of all the childish and sexist remarks. This was totally unprofessional. I was cute (in my own way) and I was very single. With this kind of support, probably for a long time.

Well, Jeff was starting with one strike against him already. I realized he had nothing to do with the broadcast but that didn't matter to me. That inner male thing took over. He was competition.

About an hour later, my boss came into my office and asked about the apartment and if I was comfortable. I let him know I could make do. I had that grin I turned into a subtle look of pain. One sacrifice after another. Dan informed me of yet another. It was only temporary, but I was getting a roommate. Great. I have work not only at the office but now waiting at home. I'm the crash and burn type of guy. I cherish my cave time and now I am losing it. Guess who my new roommate was going to be? Yah, you got it. Jeff. Strike two.

I went to his office to meet him. I knocked on his door and entered his 'Trump-style' corner office, at least three times the size of mine. Did I say three? That's right, strike three! Jeff was sitting at his desk facing the door. Smart, I thought to myself, if I were him I wouldn't have my back to the people either. I introduced myself and said, "It looks like we're going to be roommates." This was news to Jeff. He arrogantly said, "Really?" That was it, time to let him know who was in charge. "By the way," I announced, "I took the master bedroom." That seemed to fix his little red wagon.

After work we met at the apartment. Jeff seemed to be okay with it. However, he quickly pointed out the three Taco Bell bags on the kitchen counter. "What the hell is this?" Jeff asked in a very cynical manner. "They're mine, from Friday, Saturday, and Sunday.

We don't have Taco Bell in Calgary, and I love them." Jeff then informed me, "We have a stove and a fridge. I'll be cooking my food. None of this fast food crap!" Is there such a thing as strike four?

The apartment was a decent size with a nice couch and a twenty-seven-inch TV. The couch, however, was a two-seater, what's referred to as a 'love' seat. Picture Jeff and I watching the hockey game and sitting on the love seat. I was leaning as far west as possible; Jeff was leaning as far east as possible. A goal was scored and in the excitement, our knees touched. This couldn't happen! I didn't like the guy and now we were touching during the game. What would happen next? Visits in the middle of the night?

We both looked at each other in a manly way, yet each with fear in our eyes. We were going to be roommates for at least a month. This cannot happen again. Then it hit me. "Jeff, want to watch the game at Earl's (local pub)? A quick "Let's go" and we solved the problem. Thankfully they had the manly game of pool at the pub. Jeff and I (more so Jeff) controlled the table for most of the night. We made Earl's the place to go after work for the next month or so.

I had to go to Calgary the next day for work. I returned to the apartment five days later. Jeff was there but absent was that homophobic fear we both experienced that first night. There was something comforting about watching Jeff having dinner beside eight Taco Bell bags! Home run! This could be the start of a beautiful relationship!

The Wake-Up Call

Life is not a one-way street. To get to your destination you travel in many directions, very often contradicting your original path. I learned an awful lot about life at the store and applied it to my personal life. Just as frequently I would learn something in my personal life and apply that lesson to the store.

I was driving out to Vancouver Island from Calgary to visit some friends. I had a week vacation and wanted to make the best of it. Time was of the essence. I was off work early Friday afternoon and planned to be on the Island by early Saturday morning. Leaving from Calgary this meant eleven hours driving to North Vancouver to spend the night at my grandma's house. She was actually staying in Calgary visiting our family and gave me the key to her place. I would then catch the first ferry leaving Horseshoe Bay at six in the morning and arrive on the Island at my friend's place in Parksville by nine.

I left Calgary at two in the afternoon, just about an hour ahead of schedule. It's a very pleasant drive to the coast, if there is a lack of two items; snow and traffic. Since it was August, there was no snow (which is no guarantee) and leaving when I did minimized the amount of traffic. I arrived safely in North Van at just about midnight. The drive was uneventful but tiring; I had been up at 4:00 am that morning and worked a full day. So far my plan was perfect.

I got to Grandma's, the key worked, and I was inside. What a plan! I was on the bed in seconds and ready for a good sleep. I was tired enough to sleep through until lunch, but the plan was to get up in five hours. If you're ever a contestant on *Family Feud* and Richard Dawson asks you, "Name something a retired eighty two-year-old grandmother does not require." The number one answer will be, "An alarm clock!" I looked everywhere, nothing. I was so close but my plan was coming apart. Fatigue was impairing my thought process and I could sense panic beginning to creep its way into my thoughts.

Get a grip, I thought to myself. Then I had an idea. I made a phone call. A male voice on the other end of the phone said, "International Plaza Hotel North Vancouver, John here, how can I help you?" With slight apprehension, I replied, "I'd like a wake up call." John said, "Certainly sir, what room are you in?" I answered, "3738 Norwood Avenue, North Vancouver." "Sir, are you not in the hotel?" With a little explaining, John seemed sympathetic to my dilemma.

I was in one of those very deep sleeps. You know the kind, when it takes you maybe thirty seconds to figure out where you are. The ringing phone woke me up. I had a quick thrill when I realized I was in a strange bed; however, it immediately left when I remembered whose bed. I answered the phone to a cheerful voice, "Good morning, Mr. Rackham, this is John at the International Plaza Hotel with your wake-up call." I was able to catch the first ferry and my vacation ended up being great.

I used this story many times at the store when discussing service. John may have broken the first rule of wake-up calls ("Make sure they are guests staying in your hotel") but he took fifteen seconds out of his day to totally make mine. I would then ask the staff, "What could you do in fifteen seconds to make an impression on a customer?" I even took it one step further and suggested that this kind of behaviour need not be restricted to just the work place. John's act of kindness not only impacted me but also had the potential to impact thousands of people twenty five-years after the fact. Now that's a wake-up call.

A Store Divided

As you live life, you begin to realize that the quality of life you have is based solely on choices you make. What friends you hang out with, what girl you ask out, what path you choose in school, and what career you choose to follow. Every day you're faced with many choices, and every one of them could become critical as to how your life may turn out. It was a time for my employees to make a major decision: to strike or cross the picket line.

The company and the union had now been negotiating a contract for almost a year, with the present contract expired. Easter was coming up and the union figured a work stoppage just before our third largest volume week might have some impact. Our company had never been on strike before, even though the previous contract subjected the employees to considerable rollbacks in order for us to stay in business. This was considered time for a little payback. A vote was taken and the union had gotten a very strong mandate to strike. The vote was on a Sunday and the union was required to give seventy-two hours notice. This meant the picket lines would be up the Wednesday before the Easter weekend. Employees had to decide whether they were going to cross the picket line or not. As an employer, we had no idea who or how many would show up to work.

We had anticipated this turn of events and had a plan. We would only open a few stores and staff them with replacement workers, management, and employees that were willing to cross the picket line. Suddenly that plan was modified. On Monday afternoon, it was decided that every store will open regardless of their staffing situation. In other words, every store for itself! The news came from the division manager, but it was never clear who came up with the new plan. The only sure thing was it didn't come from someone actually working in the stores.

I had a staff of two hundred forty employees and not a clue who would cross the picket line. Our hiring blitz resulted in two new cashiers, but both required training.

I knew my department managers were going to cross and we had an assistant manager from Regina coming to help out. On Tuesday morning, I had two untrained kids to open on Wednesday, instead of seventy-five veteran cashiers.

This is where choices I made earlier in my life paid off. I called up an old girlfriend who used to work for us. Never burn a bridge if you don't have to. I explained the situation and she was willing to help out and even train the new cashiers. That's now three cashiers. I remembered a bartender friend of mine, whose wife worked for us a few months back. The decision to tip this bartender well paid off. His wife (I later found out she was eight months pregnant) agreed to work. That's now four! I figured we'd open up with a total of fifteen employees, instead of the two hundred forty. I remember thinking to myself, "What an opportunity to get hours!"

The new plan included working as many people to midnight as possible the day before they walked out. The thinking was to have the store absolutely can tight and piled high. We had the store looking pretty good despite of a minor 'work to rule' campaign by only a few of the employees. Actually, the employees who participated weren't working much different than they normally did. We had a few other disappointing things happen before the employees left. Some toilets were plugged (thankfully I had experience in that sort of thing) and some equipment was stolen, or temporarily misplaced. It was a very solemn feeling locking up the store. I was the last to leave what was usually a store bursting with life, as most of the work is done when the store is closed. I'm not sure customers realize how many people work after midnight. This store could have as many as thirty on a midnight shift. Tonight there was no one. I had no idea what to expect tomorrow. Employees, friends, and management would be pitted against each other, fighting for their beliefs. It was now close to 1:00 am in the morning. My normal day started at 7:00, but this was not a normal day. Three am was going to come fast.

I was back on the road at 3:30 am to pick up the only two cashiers I knew for sure that I had. It was very humbling to realize that the store could have run without me, but it couldn't without these two cashiers.

We got to the store and two more cashiers joined us as we entered. We just doubled our staff! The two experienced cashiers quickly reviewed the cash registers as they themselves required a quick refresher course, and then proceeded to turn a twenty-four hour training course into three and a half hours.

Fear is an interesting motivator. The adrenaline rush mothers experience when they see their child trapped under a car can be compared to the fear a store manager experiences when we see a hundred customers and only four cashiers. Mothers at least find some superhuman strength to lift the car off their child. A store manager's response to a hundred customers and four cashiers would be more like the movie *Psycho* where everyone is thinking, "Get out of the house!"

Eight o'clock came quickly and it was time to open the doors. There were about forty picketers and they were fired up. About ten employees walked past them to come into work and a bit of a scuffle broke out. I have never been as scared as I was opening the front doors. Could we run the store with just four cashiers? How were the picketers going to react, and how many would cross? How do you treat the picketers and how do you control all the situations that this kind of setting can create? The thought, "Get out of the house!" kept running through my mind.

After everything was said and done, opening the doors was anti-climatic. There were no customers. Gradually they trickled in at a pace we could handle. As the customer base continued to grow, so did the number of workers crossing the picket line. We never faced too many customers or not enough employees.

What I learned from the strike was the need to treat everyone, regardless of which side they took, with respect. I talked to the picketers and to the workers two to three times a day. We had an uneventful picket line, and an uneventful store. The customers expressed their opinions every time they shopped. I was very proud of all the staff during this time.

They conducted themselves professionally, minus one minor incident when the picketers pulled an elderly man out of his car. When the strike ended seventy-five days later, we were all a bit wiser and had a greater appreciation for a contract. Eventually, people forgot who said what and who crossed where. Choices made from rational thinking rather than emotion were usually the right ones, which made this period of time go much easier. I've said it before, "A strike is an experience everyone should have, but once is enough."

Picket or Kick It

"It was the best of times. It was the worst time of times," (I didn't think Chuck would mind me borrowing that line.) It was a time of many contradictions and many mixed emotions. It was 1997 and we were in our first labour dispute that I was involved in. The strike was now two days old and both sides were still very much feeling each other out. Management continued to operate the business as if there was no strike, and the strikers tested their newfound freedom by walking the picket line. This was the first time the employees could openly defy management. Neither side had experienced a strike before. Being new at it, we both fumbled our way through the beginning.

Out of two hundred forty employees, eighty crossed the picket line, eighty picketed and about eighty completely vanished (Jim Rockford on his best day couldn't have found them), not to be seen or heard from until after the strike.

It was the day before Good Friday. I was out visiting the picket line, keeping the line of communication open. I would be out five or six times a day to check on them as it was early in the strike and there wasn't much going on in the store as customers stayed away. The strike was new to our customers too. I'm sure they were uncertain of proper strike etiquette. What do you wear to a picket line crossing? How do you address the people on the picket line? Is it appropriate to tip them? If so, is ten percent of the groceries you just purchased enough?

Calgary, a heartland of right wingers, was torn. They knew that eventually these people will be packing their groceries with care, or if they pissed them off on the line, they'll be slamming their groceries without a care. Most of our customers conducted themselves like they were on a United Nations peacekeeping mission. Make no sudden movements, say nothing, and above all do not make eye contact. Pick your path to the door, put the old head down, and keep walking.

This story is about a few customers who had other plans. It was about 4:00 pm and I was chatting with the picketers. They had formed a gauntlet that had to be passed if you wanted to get in the parking lot.

A bunch of high school kids out cruising in mom's four-door Impala thought it would be cool to taunt the picketers. Because there was no school next day, it was party night! I don't know about you, but I would be hard pressed to find something more fun than antagonizing picketers. Apparently the library club must have cancelled its meeting due to the long weekend. These kids came well prepared too, with impressive lines certain to get under the skin of those tough and hardened strikers.

As they drove by, fast enough to not risk capture but slow enough to be heard, they pelted the picketers with their clever, well-constructed zingers: "Get a job!" Obviously this youth did not understand the concept of a strike. A kid from the back seat, not to be outdone, added his two cents: "Go to school, you idiots." This kid just missed a good one. He should have said 'fools.' "Go back to school, you fools." I bet he kicked himself later. Anyway the picketers' retort was no better. A quick "Oh yeah!" a couple of hand gestures, and that was it.

Then a second car drove by full of giggling teenage girls. This sent the picketers into action. Four or five of the young male picketers looked at each other. With eyes wide open and tongues dangling, they shouted, "Girls!" Then proceeded to chase after the car. A visual similar to the neighbourhood dogs chasing the butcher's truck.

The picket lines were to stay up twenty-four hours a day. At least that was the plan. After witnessing this sorry excuse for a picket line, I was pretty sure we had no graduates of the Jimmy Hoffa School of Striking.

I went to the picket captain with my concerns for the picketers' safety after hours. The picket captain was selected by the union to be responsible for the picketers.

Their mission: to ensure a peaceful yet fired up and intimidating picket line. This direction created some confusion among the picketers. It was difficult to see the line in the sand that they shouldn't cross. Some picket captains went from being a general clerk in the store with very little responsibility, to leading eighty picketers under difficult situations. Their egos swelled up while their common sense shrank.

I explained that after the store closed at nine, there were no deliveries during the night and only the stocking crew would be in the store. There would be nothing gained by picketing overnight; they'd be making themselves targets for these less-than-stellar teenagers. After about three seconds of careful consideration my request was not-so-politely turned down.

At 8:45, I was going to make my final visit with the strikers. Earlier I was e-mailed a list of about eight customers who complained the picketers were kicking their cars as they entered the parking lot. Apparently that line in the sand had shifted for some of the picketers. It was dark outside as I walked to the picket line. The parking lot, normally buzzing with activity, was almost empty. An empty parking lot to a retailer is as painful as showing up at Disneyland and it being closed.

As I approached the defiant ones, I noticed a group of teenage boys in the parking lot. At first I thought customers, then replacement workers! That pipe dream lasted as long as it took me to see the bats, pipes, and sticks they were carrying. I asked the strikers if they knew them. The reply was, "No, but they seem to know us." This was what I was afraid of. There were six kids. Five carrying items that I believed were not going to be used as they were originally intended. The sixth kid didn't have a weapon; he didn't need one, as he was obviously kin to Andre the Giant.

Like the picket captain, my common sense suffered from shrinkage. I told the picketers to stay put, and I walked out to the strike-breakers. They were huddled around Mom's Impala that was parked under the light. I very firmly said, "Can I help you guys?"

A kid of medium size with lots of red hair answered back, "They kicked my car, now we're going to kick their asses!" I remembered the list. I pulled it from my pocket and scanned the names. The first name on the list was a Trevor. If I ever imagined what a Trevor would look like, this kid would be it. I looked him straight in the eye, "Are you Trevor?" The kid gave that deer in the headlight look. Bingo! Looking him dead in the eye, "I've got your name and number, we'll be in touch. Now you're on private property. You have no business here. You and your friends get in your car and leave. You're not welcome here."

What happened next was as big a surprise to me as it was to everyone on the line. These five kids took their bats and sticks, climbed in the car and drove off without a peep. Yep, don't mess with my staff or you'll have to mess with me! The sixth kid, the big one, was still there. I just handled five, what's one more? "Have you got a problem?" I very firmly asked him. I had a brief flashback of Robert De Niro in Taxi. "Are you talking to me?" The kid, up close, strangely resembled an adult. He looked at me and stated, "I'm Constable MacIntire. "I was just talking to these youths and had already asked them to leave the area." I had a look on my face that I usually saved for the socks I would get for Christmas. "So you're telling me I didn't do this?" The constable could see my disappointment. "You did very well though." I asked him what he was doing there. He wasn't in uniform. "I was just picking up a few groceries and saw these kids looking for trouble." I thanked him as we both chuckled.

While I was walking with him back to the store, I asked, "You mind not saying anything about this to the picketers?" He laughed and said, "Not a problem." I was thinking this man has a brilliant future ahead of him as I walked through the picket line to a chorus of, "Way to go, Dave, you're the man!" And even a few high fives. Perception can be a beautiful thing. And even better yet, knowing when to be silent!

Truth or Consequences

As the competition continued to grow in our industry, so did the expectations of the employees in the stores. To stay price competitive and still turn a profit, expenses in the stores had to be cut. At first it was easy, like swinging a machete through the rain forests. There were lots to cut. However, after a few years of this constant reducing, we required a skilled surgeon with a scalpel to cut any more. The brunt of the pressure fell on the employees. Management had higher expectations while at the same time much lower compensation for the staff. This combination did not help employee attendance reach the stellar levels achieved when I was part-time. I could empathize with the employees, but my job was to ensure a properly staffed operation so that we could run our business effectively. In other words, if you miss a shift, you better have a valid reason, and if questioned be prepared to substantiate your reason.

It was a Saturday (imagine that), when I took a phone call from a part-time cashier, Kerry. It was about noon, his shift was at 3:30 pm, and yes, he was too ill to work. I asked him, "Are you sure you couldn't struggle through a shift? Saturday night is impossible to replace." Kerry replied, "I'm dying, there's no way." All I could do was say, "Fine, see me next time you're in." I always thought that would scare them straight.

Helena, one of the customer service people who look after the front started at two o'clock. She was perusing the daily (the list of cashier assignments), and noticed Kerry's name removed from the list. "Why is Kerry's name scratched off the list?" I explained he was sick. Helena looked at me with a perplexed expression. "He didn't look sick fifteen minutes ago when I saw him at Starbucks." With that information, I said to myself, "Game on." I called Kerry's home, and asked to speak to him. His mother explained he was out for the afternoon. I asked if she knew when he would be back. "I have no idea," she said. "Who may I say is calling?" "It's Dave calling from the store." Well, this lady didn't get her money's worth from Arthur Murray's School of Dance. "Oh the store...he's...at the...doctor. He went to the doctor." At best, a very uninspiring dance. I simply replied, "That's great, just have Kerry call me when he gets in."

Well, there was no return call, not a surprise or a big deal. Kerry was most likely using the 'delay and pray' technique: put as much time between the crime and the next meeting, and pray the manager forgets. Such as "I know he did something, but for the life of me I can't remember what!" Or, "I know someone called in sick who wasn't, but for the life of me I can't remember who!"

Kerry worked the following Thursday and I was ready for him with the shop steward. If I was going to discipline him, I was required to have a union representative present. He'd have a little explaining to do. When he started his shift, I invited him to my office. Kerry came in and sat down in front of my desk, and in a very up-beat manner asked, "What's up?" "Kerry, I need you to explain what happened last Saturday." "Oh the day I was sick. Well, I was feeling so bad I didn't think it would be right to come into work, possibly infecting someone else. I went to my doctor on Saturday. It was going to be an hour wait so I went to Starbucks to get a coffee. It sometimes settles my stomach. Oh, by the way, I saw Helena there too." Boy, this kid is good. Now he got his money's worth from Arthur Murray's.

After Kerry finished, I gave him the old "sounds good but my gut just doesn't buy it." He swore this was what happened. By contract, we have the right to ask for medical confirmation. I asked Kerry to provide a note that would substantiate his medical appointment. I didn't want a note saying he was sick; I needed a note that stated he had an appointment that Saturday. Kerry said, "No problem, but a note will cost me ten dollars." I added, "If you bring a note confirming the appointment, I'll pay for it and I'll give you my most sincere apology."

The next day Kerry came to my office with a smile and a note. He seemed very pleased with himself. I read the note and it confirmed he was sick that Saturday, not that he had an appointment. I explained this was not what I had asked. Kerry replied that, "The doctor said it would do." I said, "Do you mind if I call your doctor?" "Help yourself," he replied as he went to work.

It was Friday of the May long weekend when I called the medical office and got a recording that said they were closed for the holiday weekend. I dialled again and asked my assistant to listen to the recording, only I got a real person this time.

I explained to the receptionist who I was and what I needed. She very politely stated that this was confidential information. I explained I didn't need any medical information just the appointment. No dice. I thanked her for her time and said I understood. Just before I hung up this lady asked, "Do you have any other questions?" I thought for a moment then something occurred to me! "Are you open on the weekends?" I asked. "No we are not," was the reply. "Any chance you were open last Saturday?" "Absolutely not!" was the receptionist's answer. Game, set and match!

Well I asked the shop steward to get Kerry and bring him back to the office. I had shared my findings with the steward and explained that I would offer him a mulligan, a chance to do it over, but I had better get the truth. It all worked out; Kerry came clean. There's something satisfying about humbling the odd employee who thinks they put one over on you. A wise person once told me to always have a questioning attitude.

Colouring Outside the Lines

Almost every year I tried to have an Easter colouring contest for the kids. The store would provide an Easter scene to be coloured by the kids, split up into three age groups: under six, six to eight, and nine to ten. Each age group would get one winner selected by a panel of judges. The winners would receive a thirty-second shopping spree using one of our 'mini' buggies. These 'mini' buggies were in the store to help teach the kids proper shopping etiquette and safety in the store. When pushing their buggy around, they would be angels, mimicking Mom or Dad, cautious and courteous. Of course, it all could have been a ploy to sell more band-aids; the buggy had the ability to remove skin when unexpected contact was made. Especially in the ankle area!

It was always impressive to see all the artwork, usually about five hundred pieces. A psychologist could have a field day analyzing the colours chosen by some of the kids and the intensity of the grip used on the crayon. I suspected that some of these kids had issues. The parents would bring the grandparents or any family member they could persuade into the store to show off the work of their budding Bateman or potential Picasso. This was good business.

There was one contest that stood far above the others. To maximize community involvement, I went to the local seniors' home and solicited six residents to judge the contest. Make no mistake; these people took the role seriously. To the point that I got a phone call one week prior to the contest judging, asking what the proper attire to wear was.

The contest closed Thursday and the judges came at 9:00 am on Good Friday. We set up the coffee room to be 'Contest Central.' The energy expended by the seniors was unprecedented. Just to keep up their strength, they required three dozen donuts, two litres of orange juice, and two pots of decaffeinated coffee, all double doubles. They were in their fourth hour of judging, when I was certain I heard one of them mention the possibility of being 'sequestered.'

Time for me to take charge. With a little encouragement, we finally got three winners. Of course, not without the authenticity of some of the work coming under scrutiny. Seniors can be a suspicious lot. Eventually everyone was happy with the selections. The winners' efforts were clearly evident. The pride put into these pieces of art was undeniable.

Now for the fun of informing the winners of the contest. I carefully planned this portion. I believed that the kids will remember this along with their other most cherished memories. When I called their home I asked for them personally. I knew this would concern the parents just enough so that they would hang by the phone to see what was up and inevitably see their child's face light up with the news. This way the kids got to inform the parents, a real treat for any kid. The parents all eventually got on the phone and I informed them of the particulars, one parent twice, as they were as excited as their kids were! Never underestimate the power of a colouring contest with a thirty-second shopping spree attached.

It was the morning of the shopping spree and the crowds were beginning to filter into the store. The electricity was flowing through the building, exciting even the most hardened veterans of past colouring contests. The three winners were easy to pick; as they were the best-behaved kids and the only ones floating into the store. We had the winning artwork displayed prominently at the front of the store. Yes, these three young people were stars.

I gathered the contestants with their parents to explain the rules of the spree. I remember looking at these parents and thinking if their kids ever win an Olympic gold medal it might just be a letdown to what they're feeling today. I was a little worried about all this emotion affecting the performances of the three shoppers. These children didn't have the advantages of the kids today utilizing a sports physiologist for the event.

The rules were simple: start at the check stand, I say go, and you fill up your basket with as much as you can for thirty-seconds. The first contestant was a five-year-old boy.

On 'go' he went right to the candy aisle, filling his basket with as much as he could. However, the pressure got to him. He became indecisive and actually froze for a moment, killing valuable seconds. The final tally: $14.00. You could see the disappointment in his eyes, but he was brave and didn't say anything.

The second contestant was a seven-year-old girl. The coaching was very evident here. On 'go,' she went straight to the detergent aisle, picked up a box of Tide, then without hesitation headed to the Meat department and picked up a prime rib roast.

Her mission was completed and she headed for home. I thought about this for a while, trying to put a positive note on it. Perhaps this was Sunday dinner, the daughter sitting in Dad's usual chair and the meal dedicated to the contest winner. I would be okay with that.

The third and final contestant was a ten-year-old boy. He had the savvy of someone who had been in this position before. Maybe not a colouring contest, but possibly a science fair, certainly at least show and tells. On the word, he headed down the candy aisle, very cognizant of the time, ten seconds, and then off to the variety aisle. This was different; this aisle contained light bulbs, automotive, school supplies, and other things of that nature. This kid had done his homework. He must have scouted the store out the night before, because he found the best item in the store. Even I was envious of his pick. An official National Hockey League-sanctioned Don Cherry hockey trading card album with extra sleeves. That reminded me of a catch phrase some of the older managers use to tell us, 'Prior planning prevents poor performances.'

When the first kid (the five-year-old) saw this, his jaw dropped to the floor and his eyes started watering. He looked at me and said, "I didn't know you had that." All I could say was, "To be honest, kid, neither did I!" Looking at his somewhat dismal collection of candy, I motioned over to the variety manager and asked her to do something for me. Seconds later she walked up to the brave but disillusioned five year old and put an official NHL-sanctioned Don Cherry hockey trading card album with extra sleeves in his basket.

This kid looked at me and said, "I don't deserve this, I don't." He started looking around the store, I thought for his mother, but he eventually saw what he was looking for. He took his basket and wheeled it up to the Food Bank bin. Without any prompting, he put all his candy into the bin.

I was stunned. I had to take a moment to comprehend what had happened. This youngster, caught up in a celebration for his talents, was still grounded enough to think of others. This offering, which is rarely seen without a lot of extrinsic forces motivating the individual, immediately silenced the crowd, leaving them staring at each other in disbelief.

I will never underestimate the power of a colouring contest, and even more so the power of a child. This unnamed five-year-old boy, who made such a profound gesture, impacted my thinking and gave me confidence that the world just may have a strong future. To the parents of that remarkable kid, well done.

The Carry Out

It baffles me that whenever I talk about shoplifting in a grocery store most people are shocked that anyone would want to steal anything from us. They seem to believe that only department stores have anything worth stealing. Pride is a funny thing. I often found myself selling the idea of shoplifting in my store. Anything the department stores can do, we can do better!

I had two rules regarding shoplifting. One, if I ever caught someone stealing a loaf of bread because they were hungry, I would throw in some meat for a proper sandwich. Jean Valjean's (Les Miserables) story always stuck with me: the gentleman in France who got twenty-five years in prison for stealing a loaf of bread. However, in over thirty years, no one ever stole a loaf of bread. They were hungrier for beef tenderloin, shrimp, batteries, DVDs, and razor blades.

Two, if I ever caught a kid stealing condoms, I would ask him why he needed them. If the answer was because they make the best water bombs, then he would have to deal with the repercussions. If it was because he wanted to be responsible but was nervous buying them, I would just get the money from him and send him on his way.

This was a particularly bad week for shoplifting. It seemed like we were free game for anyone without talent or unwilling to put out any effort. Just come in the store, load up, and get out. If they knew we spotted them, the product would be dropped and the shoplifter would leave the store, very often with a single finger salute.

It was just before lunch, and one of the clerks alertly informed me of two shoplifters loading up with meat. One was the lookout while the other was filling his pants, shirt and jacket. No matter how often we're put in this situation, our adrenaline starts pumping and our excitement usually gives us away. One clerk went to the door so the thief with the meat couldn't make a run for it. The lookout saw us and got out; as saving himself was his priority.

I was told the fellow with the meat went down the freezer aisle. As I was heading down the aisle, I could see this guy pulling package after package out of his various hiding places.

When I came up behind him, I was pissed. This ass had about ten packages of meat he had already dropped on the floor. Since he hadn't left the store I couldn't arrest him for shoplifting. What I could do, however, was help him out of the store.

I grabbed him by his collar and the back of his belt. "Is that all of it?" I asked. He replied, "Yes," as I turned him around, heading for the door. I informed him he was no longer welcome in the store. I added, "This'll be a walk in the park compared to what will happen if you try this again." I remembered a situation I was once in, when I got enthusiastically escorted out of a nightclub through a set of doors that weren't open. At least not until I opened them with my head. I added, "You better pray the doors open, 'cause either way you're going through!" I must have been fairly scary because as I assisted this gentleman in leaving the store, he took the initiative to run the rest of the way out of the parking lot.

I was visibly shaken, as I'm not used to being that angry. One of the clerks, looking at me in amazement, informed me that the shoplifter's feet never touched the floor. I realized that this incident would get through the store and probably grow some legs of its own. It doesn't hurt for the staff to realize you do have a limit. "Walk softly and carry a big stick, but if you never swing that big stick you're just walking softly." Without saying anything, the staff was extra attentive and accommodating to me. This new respect lasted for about a week. Life is good when a negative can be turned into a positive. If you can use a shoplifter for that purpose, then it's a real bonus. However, if anybody is reading this story and thinking about shoplifting in a grocery store, don't do it. The department stores have a much better selection!

The Ugly Duckling

Managers are frequently required to transfer stores. Sometimes for a promotion, sometimes a demotion, sometimes you were thrilled and sometimes disappointed. The only certainty was that you were moving. These moves weren't debated or negotiated. Many hours committed by many people, planning strategies, career paths, and store needs go into every set of moves. There was purpose and reason behind every move. Actually, many of us speculated that upper management found out where you lived and then located the store furthest from that point.

Still, we went to the new store that another manager ran and then proceeded to take over the operation, trying not to offend the previous manager or shake up the staff too much. Everyone runs their store differently. I always thought that every manager should watch an old Humphrey Bogart movie, *The Caine Mutiny*. It demonstrated the effects two different management styles had on people, and can have on a team. Bogart's character, Captain Queeg, was a World War II naval captain who was a strict disciplinarian. He was replacing an easier going captain, but one who still got results. Captain Queeg says, "You tell the men there are four ways of doing things on this ship: the right way, the wrong way, the navy way, or my way. If you do things my way we'll get along just fine!" The important thing was that you took ownership of the store and made the store yours. If you went to a store that you were not happy going to, this could be difficult. You can fool your boss but you can never fool the staff. They'll always see you for what you are.

I was managing a small store in an upper-class part of town. The president of the company lived nearby and shopped my store regularly. An honour, but in reality it was a pain in the butt. I remember customers using his name to try and get special privileges. "I am good friends with your president" or "I live next door to your president." I heard these comments so many times that one afternoon a customer claimed to be our president's next door neighbour. I replied, "I've got to see his house, it must be very unique."

The customer, in a boorish manner questioned, "Why?" "You're the thirty-seventh person to tell me you're his next door neighbour. He must have the strangest looking house to have that many next door neighbours!" As usual my timing was a little off. This was our president's next-door neighbour.

It wasn't long thereafter that I was transferred to another store. An older store, less volume, and in an area of town that I considered much less desirable. When the district manager explained where I was going, I voiced my displeasure, while still maintaining some level of professionalism. It didn't matter, the move was done. I was told on Friday and started at the new store on Sunday.

That Sunday was a dull, gray February day, the kind of day you just want to curl up and watch an old black and white movie. Instead I'm in the parking lot of this old, neglected, and tired store. The parking lot can be a good indicator of what your clientele will be like. I left BMWs and Range Rovers and traded them for rusted, Country Squire station wagons and a bicycle with a pit bull tied to it.

The store was located in Bowness, very close to the Bow River. Actually a very picturesque part of town, but considered a tough area due to the occasional murder, and the fact it was selected as the place to live by two of Calgary's most popular bike gangs. My district manager referred to this store as "Bowghetto." This was the store I was going to have to call my own. I disliked everything about it, from the diarrhea brown paint on the outside trim to the safe that had a round door. If the shape of the safe door bothered me, I must have been pissed. My first customer was an inebriated man needing cigarettes, one pack at a time. I was not anticipating a large amount of full carton sales. As I gradually met the thirty-eight staff members I recall thinking of them as the misfits. All the employees banished by other stores buried here, including me.

I wasn't very happy the first few weeks, but gradually that changed. I found it takes a lot more energy to be miserable than happy. One small event at a time started to change my opinion of my prison term.

A good friend and produce merchandiser at the time, Ewen, noticed my frustration and disappointment in my new assignment. Ewen thought of how he could cheer me up and decided that a few beers were in order. As if that would help! Well, it couldn't hurt.

He took me across the street to the Royal Canadian Legion. If you've never been in a Legion, it's worth a visit. They're like a pub in a museum, or even better, drinking a cold, frosty one, during history class. As I walked in I suddenly realized why we sold more cigarettes at the store than we did meat.

The smoke was so thick in this place that you couldn't see across the room. I felt like a character in an old western: a stranger walking into the saloon. Everybody stopped what he or she was doing to see who the new folks were. They looked at us and I guess decided we were okay, then continued to inhale smoke and swallow beer at the same time.

We were just sitting down for a drink when a gruff old gentleman came over for a closer look. "Say, aren't you the new Safeway store manager?" I simply replied, "Yes." The gentleman's eyes widened and he shouted across the bar to another elderly man playing pool, "Charlie, it's the new Safeway store manager!" At that point everyone turned to take a second look. Charlie came over carrying his pool cue and shook my hand. He introduced Sam, the gentleman who spotted me. During the two beers Ewen and I had just about everyone come over to say hi. It's amazing how a little stroking of the ego can lift your spirits. That day I officially became a "Big fish in a small pond," a very small pond, but my pond nevertheless.

It was time to get this store, my store and the employees' store, in shape. First thing to do was to strip the floors of the hundred or so layers of dirty old wax and put down fresh wax. Ten of us did it on a Sunday night and were blown away by how spectacular the floors came up. The shine was simply brilliant. Next was to paint the inside of the store. The walls were covered by the old sixties style wood grain mac-tac. Very dark and very dated. We selected an eggshell white, which gave the store a very bright, clean, and fresh look. Our florist hung some silk plants along the bulkheads and the inside of the store now had a warm and inviting look.

We had style; we were just missing attitude! We had to be proud of our store. I told this to the staff and they ate it up. In two weeks everybody would answer the phone, "Safeway on the Bow." They all cared about the store and worked hard to maintain it. At my last store the customers expected a great store and service. I now realized that these Bowness customers were different; they appreciated a great store and service.

My district manager held the weekly meeting at our store. I felt bad, as we weren't set up for a meeting. We had no boardroom, just a coffee room, with two picnic tables to sit at. Afterwards, I asked why he had the meeting here. He looked at me with a slightly devious smile and said, "I wanted the managers to see what a forty-year-old store could look like." It's hard to believe that just a little comment like that could have moved me so much. At that moment I must have got something in my eye. That can happen in our industry.

Whatever you do, wherever you go, it's not the outside forces that affect you. The location, condition, or the size of the store is insignificant. The location of your mind set, the condition of your heart, and the size of your commitment is what will determine your experience. It's all up to the choices you make.

There was the Montreal Canadiens of the fifties,
the New York Yankees of the seventies
and then the Bowness employees of the eighties!

Swifter Higher Stronger

The workplace is the ultimate investment that will give you the greatest return. I firmly believe the more effort you put into your work, the more you will get out. I'm not necessarily talking monetary rewards, although it is important to be compensated fairly, but if that's all you get from your job you're cheating yourself. You should get a feeling of accomplishment, recognition from supervisors, respect from your peers, and the ability to look at a job well done and feel a satisfaction that only requires your approval. I had the opportunity to meet the president of the company early in my career. He gave me some great advice that I have lived by: "Always be happy where you're at, but not necessarily content."

It was always interesting to see brand new employees, most of them working for the first time, starting to define themselves in the work place. I often wondered if any of them had a plan for their interview similar to mine. A few quick answers and I'm out of here! Or did they really want the job? Either way, they're working now. It wasn't hard to identify the people who can be given more responsibility. Initiative, dependability, positive attitude, and a work ethic will get you moving up. When we identified individuals to promote, they often had to leave their friends behind.

A newly promoted cashier asked me if he could talk to me in private. "Absolutely, let's go to my office." Brent explained to me that he wanted to go back to courtesy clerk. I asked him why. He explained that he was uncomfortable giving direction to the courtesy clerks. I began to suspect another reason. A few well-placed questions and the truth came out. His friends were giving him a rough time. A very common occurrence. It seemed that it was the right time for a story.

It was 1967, Canada's centennial year. I was in grade three training very hard for the national fitness test. This was a series of exercises, sit ups, push ups, standing broad jump, arm hang, and running, with your results measured and then rewarded with a bronze, silver, or gold maple leaf crest. To earn gold you had to be gold in all disciplines. One slip up, a silver or bronze in any one sport, and that was the level you were awarded.

There was a reason I wanted gold so badly; it was more than pride, and even more than the glory. It was Barbara, a cute and athletic girl in my class. If I could just get a gold maple leaf patch, then maybe she would notice me. I trained as hard as a grade three could. After school I would have competitions with my sister and brother. Mom and Dad would hold our feet for the sit-ups, counting and encouraging us all. When the week came for testing, I was ready.

After the first four events, I was gold in all of them. All that was left was the three hundred-yard run. I was the fastest runner in my class. This last event was a sure thing. I was running the race and in great position with the finish line about fifty yards ahead, when I heard a friend call out, "Dave, wait up for me." It was Eric, the most popular kid in the class. He was held back a year so he was one year older. He was 'The Fonz' before there was an Arthur Fonzarelli. This very cool kid wanted me to slow down for him! You better believe I slowed down. As I did, I noticed my arch enemy, Tommy run by (everyone in the third grade has an arch enemy). Well, Eric caught up and we crossed the finish line together, one second too slow to get the gold! Almost forty years later and I can still hear the words and feel the sharp pain in my heart when Barbara stood up in the class and said, "We should all applaud Tommy, as he was the only one to get a gold patch."

I could see Brent was reflecting on my story, and gradually a light seemed to go on inside his head. Now it was not a halogen bulb, it was more like an energy-saving, sixty-watt bulb, but a light nevertheless. He looked at me and said, "I'll stay in the job. Thanks for the story, it really opened my eyes." I thought to myself, finally, one of my stories hit home. Now that's what managing is all about. Two weeks later I got Brent's resignation letter. You can paint a picture, lay it all out, but when the rubber hits the road, the individual will decide their own path.

The only time I couldn't find the silver lining of the story, the silver patch yes, the lining no.

A River Runs Through It

Sunday dinner at the folks is a tradition in our family. With six very different personalities, we don't always hang out together. We do, however, all regard Sunday dinner as a must, not because we have to, but because we want to. All of us are somewhat opinionated and are willing to back our beliefs. Our spirited debates are often fueled by our genuine passion and a little wine or beer.

My brother Jim and I often sat on opposite sides of the dinner table, usually debating union versus non-union, or management versus labourer. Jim works for the City of Calgary Water Works trouble crew. The constant stereotyping of city workers was always a sensitive issue with him. I was careful to steer away from that topic, but in the back of my mind I had kept it stored ready to use in a crisis. That would be if I was losing the debate.

It was a Monday morning in the store and I was minutes away from opening our doors, when John our utility clerk came running up front shouting, "There's a leak in the back room! There's a leak in the back room!" I stopped him and said, "John, there's no need to panic. Show me the leak and we'll figure out what to do." John was still overly excited as he took me to the back room. I kept saying to him, "Relax, it's no big deal, we've had leaks before."

He took me to the compressor room and said, "It's in there." As I was about to open the doors to the room, John backed away. He knew something I didn't. The doors flew open and I was met with a tsunami. A wave of water at least a foot and a half tall washed through the back room. I realized this was not a significant wave in Hawaii, but as back rooms go, it was a good size. If you've been to Niagara Falls and heard the sound of millions of tons of water flowing over the falls, it would be comparable to what I was hearing. My natural reaction was to close the doors. I leaned against the doors, visualizing the rising water and the electric engines running in the compressor room. The water and the electric… "Open the doors!" I screamed and was met by a second tsunami wave. I was told those waves always travel in pairs.

Our water main had broken and it was sending water into the store, coming up from the ground with the equivalence of three fire hoses. Pete, my assistant, came to the scene. I told him to get the benches from the coffee room and we'd channel most of the water through the back room and into the loading dock where we had a drain. The assistant in the store is usually the "get down and dirty" worker. Pete asked, "What about my new shoes?" I pretended I didn't hear that.

At this point the water had already gone right through the entire store and was flowing out the front doors. It was then I noticed that the water possessed a slightly murky quality. I called the City Water Works for help. I had one of the cashiers put signs on the doors explaining that the store was temporarily closed. I got back on the phone to inform the district manager of our situation. Pete again asked me about his shoes. At that point one of the tilt back displays fell over. A tilt back display is a temporary cardboard displayer with impulse items on them. We had twenty of these positioned around the store. It was like the domino effect, the first one fell then immediately a second, then a third, until they all fell into the muddy waters.

Within minutes of my call, the water works trouble truck pulled up to the front of my store and out jumped my favorite brother Jim! He very calmly surveyed the situation and concluded it was a water main break! Utter brilliance. Jim, with a massive wrench in hand went to the back of the store and turned off our water. He was just missing a red cape. Again, Pete asked me about his shoes. After witnessing Pete's performance in the heat of the moment, I felt a change in his introduction was required. "Jim, this is Pete, he is a general clerk in the store."

Jim gave me some pointers on cleaning up the mess and he called to get a crew to repair the damaged water main. The store opened at 3:00 pm that day, with shiny floors. I thanked John for his quick reaction to our 'leak' and introduced him to the term 'subterranean waterways.' I discussed Pete's performance with him and told him I didn't feel he was committed to the position and he agreed. As for his shoes, I offered him a very well broken in pair of Basketmaster running shoes!

This experience gave me a great appreciation for my brother's job. It is very reassuring that his crew is there when you need them. So, city workers, lean on that shovel for a moment if you want. I know when we need you, you'll be there!

My Pal Brice

Every store has an employee's kid who becomes a part of the store's personality. These are the ones who get excited when going to Mom or Dad's work place. There isn't one particular thing that makes these children stand out above the rest, but rather a series of events. Through time and consistency of behavior, these children make a mark in your life. No matter what happens or how much time passes, their mark will not fade.

My pal Brice is one of those kids. Brice was two when I first met him. His mom, Christine, was a cashier at our store and his dad, worked with me a few years earlier at another store. I believe that children, like animals, have the ability to sense qualities in people. Lassie always knew who was the good guy and who was the bad guy and would wag her tail or growl accordingly. Brice would insist on his parents taking him to see me every time he was in the store and he only growled at me once. I will admit, he could have only been interested in the security camera that I controlled from my office. Brice got a kick out of seeing his image on the monitor.

We went through a routine every time we met. I would get him to shake my hand and dare him to out squeeze me. This was standard Uncle 101 "let him win" philosophy. Brice would stick his head around the corner of the door with a grin as big as his face would allow and then pretend to play shy. No matter what though, we always shook hands and Brice always got me to my knees squeezing the life out of me.

One Halloween, Christine, brought him to the store. Brice stuck his head in my door and even though he was a ghost, I could recognize his three-foot frame from under the costume. Here he was, all giggles and smiles, with sac in hand and holding it out for me to fill it with candies. This seemed a little too easy. It finally dawned on me what was really happening. Brice wasn't holding his sac out for me to put candies in; he was holding it out offering me his candies. Way to go, Brice! I see nothing wrong with taking candy from a baby. Heck, I was likely doing him a favour. While I was looking for my favourite Halloween candies (Rockets), Christine explained to me what was going on.

They believed that before Brice goes out to ravage and pillage the neighbourhood, similar to the crusades through Europe, he must first learn how good it feels to give. Brice laughed and giggled his way around the store not like a ghost, but more like Santa, giving candy to everyone.

Here was an example of parents actually parenting their kids. Offer your kids every experience possible. Don't assume they'll only appreciate the conventional activities we expect. Let them pick and choose from a wide variety of experiences. I'm certain the end result will be an adult who is an individual that has learned to enjoy life by living it.

Brice is now eight and I'm told last Halloween he cut trick or treating off early so he could man the door at home giving the candy out. That's my pal Brice.

It Takes a Thief

This is a story that I am finding very difficult to write. It was a dark period of my life. I was confused, rebellious towards authority and I had a hunger that needed satisfying at any cost, no matter who I hurt. I was four years old and wanted a piece of candy, and I wanted it now!

I was with my mom in the neighbourhood grocery store in North Vancouver. While she was looking for nutritious food to feed her family, I was surveying the bulk candy to feed that sugar-craving demon deep within me. I realized that as a four year old my options were limited. I either had to depend on the kindness of others, or put a plan together that would allow me to satisfy that hunger, on my terms, yet go undetected. This was my first time attempting such an endeavour, but I had an idea. When no one was looking, I thought to myself, grab it! I had the target selected: a cherry flavoured hard candy with the chewy centre that was to die for! It was on a display that was open for anyone to take, almost like they dared you. I accepted the challenge!

The key to my plan was simple but effective. I was always a believer in simplicity, and that's all a four year old is really capable of. The key was timing. I waited by the display. Easy, Dave. Wait, wait, not yet. My mom was looking in the dairy aisle, trying to find the freshest quart of milk. I had the green light! Without hesitation I smoothly palmed the candy as if I had done it hundreds of times before. Now, to feast on my plunder! I unwrapped the candy and began to enjoy it very carefully, almost seductively, if that's possible for a four year old. I savoured the moment, likening it to a fisherman enjoying his catch or a hunter his kill.

All that was left to make my felony the perfect crime was to get rid of the evidence. I had been taught not to litter, though come to think of it, I had also been taught not to steal. Apparently, only the littering thing stuck. I had to find a place to unload the wrapper. I knew I was running out of time. Mom had made her choice, placed the milk in the basket and was now leading us to the checkouts.

I couldn't for the life of me find a garbage can. This was not good. My mom noticed my hand. "What have you got there?" she asked. I thought for a moment. All I had was a piece of paper, why should I worry? I opened my palm, exposing the wrapper. She knew I ate the candy. That 'little birdie' had squealed on me again. Mom often told us kids that "a little birdie told me." That bird was responsible for my apprehension in many of my other escapades. Lucky we never ran into each other. I owed him.

When it came to discipline, my mom was very creative. Since her first lesson on stealing didn't take, she tried another avenue. I saw the disappointment in her face while she was explaining my crime to the cashier. I wanted to hide, but she placed me directly in front of the cashier, who then proceeded to give me the lecture of a lifetime. I don't recall the exact words, but I found the right path in a hurry.

I never forgot my time on the wrong side of the law, regardless of how brief the term. Throughout my career I must have given hundreds of lectures to the sugar-demon- possessed kids of today. Most of the kids we caught were using my original plan. It had lost its lustre after seeing just how poorly it worked. I quickly turned my thinking from creating the perfect crime to creating the perfect story, one that would set these kids on the right path, away from a life of crime.

The cashier who took the time to set me straight deserves a big thank you. I wonder if she had someone who had straightened her out. After all, sometimes it takes a thief to know a thief.

Colonel Mustard With the Revolver in the Library

Thursday was boys' night out. About six of us from the company and a few from outside the company would meet at a local gathering place and share our stories of the week. It was comforting to know that the problems in your store were much the same as everyone else's. Not enough hours, not enough skilled help, and constantly changing expectations would be the topic of conversation for the first hour, then we would get into the good stuff: cloth diapers versus disposable, extra pulp or no pulp, hardwood versus tile. The more varied the conversation, the greater the escape.

Thursday was a good night to gallivant, as I did not have to be at work until noon on Friday. I arrived home at 1:30 am rid of the stress that had built up during the week and a few hundred dollars from a side trip to the casino. While drinking my orange juice (no pulp), I turned on my answering machine: "Dave, it's Kim from the store. Everything's all right, the police just left." Now that's comforting! Message two: "Hello, Dave, this is Steven from security. Your store was robbed at gunpoint last night. Everyone is okay but we have a few concerns. We need to meet first thing this morning." I called the store and talked to the lead person on the night crew. A kid with a gun had robbed the express checkout. In and out very quick, taking about a thousand dollars and leaving a terrified sixteen-year-old cashier.

In our industry, first thing in the morning is 6:00 am. My day was going to start very soon! I got to bed at a little after two and got up at five. You don't think about robberies very often as they very seldom occur in our area. Sometimes this can create a very casual attitude towards them. The night, along with the drive to work, was spent thinking of all the things that could have gone wrong. You begin to question yourself and wonder, did I screw up?

I got to work as the sun was just breaking the horizon. As I was walking from my parking spot to the store, my shadow was about twenty feet long. I felt more like twenty inches.

I beat security to the store so I did my own investigation as to the possible concerns. When Bonnie (the cashier) was robbed, she gave him all her cash, called the manager to the express checkout for assistance, then proceeded to take the next order. I admired her dedication, but told her she should have shouted for help, made a scene.

After I reviewed the actions taken by the employees involved, it became apparent that during a robbery the thinking process becomes very impaired. Normally simple actions become very arduous. Actions that should have been clear were complicated by the influx of adrenaline. The store required a complete review and simplification of the necessary actions to be implemented in case of a robbery. At least we gained something positive from the theft.

Bonnie, however, would not return to work. She gave her resignation, which I refused to accept. It took two weeks before she would talk to me. When she did, I told her that I would like her to at least use our counselling services before she resigned. These types of incidents are very frightening and can surface later as post-traumatic stress syndrome. If after she met with a counsellor she still wanted to quit, I would accept her resignation and date the termination back to the original request. Bonnie agreed and the appointment was made.

While I was trying to look after our employee, the police were trying to solve the crime. The suspect was caught on the store camera: a teenage boy, medium size, with a brand-new pair of Nike running shoes that seemed to glow in the dark. The constables who did the initial investigation that night were still on patrol when they received a noise complaint over the computer. One of the constables thought the address looked familiar. She checked her notebook and saw that it was the home address of the cashier who was robbed. They decided to investigate the noise complaint themselves and found a party going on. When discussing the noise issue with Bonnie, the constables noticed a teenage boy, medium size, with a brand new pair of Nike running shoes that seemed to glow in the dark.

Well, it didn't take much detective work to figure out that the teenage boy's name, most likely would be 'Clyde.' It turned out Bonnie's boyfriend was the assailant and the two had planned the robbery together. This news was very distressing. Bonnie was not a bad kid, just with the wrong crowd. Bonnie wrote a letter to me apologizing for her actions. In the letter she stated, "My mother raised me to be a good person, be honest, and kind. These people were fun to be with; I felt I was in an 'in crowd', guess not. If I could turn back time I would have picked my friends and choices more wisely. I should've known from the beginning to say see you later to these friends I had."

I've thought about the situation this young person was in, and it occurred to me that she was never given the tools to prevent herself or get herself out of a situation like this. I believe we are taught both in the school and at home how to be a good leader, but fail to admit that we will all at some point be required to follow. We need to teach our children what characteristics to look for in a leader or a friend. We need to give the tools that will enable them to withstand peer pressure and get themselves out of bad situations. Or better yet, prevent them from getting into these scenarios in the first place. I'm not sure where Bonnie is today. If she meant what she wrote, she'll be fine.

Earth, Wind, and Fire

To a grocer, the single most powerful word that will generate anticipation and excitement -- and at the same time apprehension and fear -- is 'remodel.' A store needs to regenerate itself every five to seven years. We must be in tune with the trends and be willing to take chances and start trends of our own. You want your store to differentiate itself from your competitors. A facelift is the most dramatic and clear message a store can send to customers to show that we are committed to being the place to shop.

Tamara Johnston

Our store was selected for a major remodel, which included an addition of ten thousand square feet, the relocating of almost all departments, a complete new look to the exterior, and adding a second entranceway, all badly needed and long over due. It was to start in August and finish five

Now this was an extreme makeover

months later in December. At least that was the plan.

During the remodel, a manager loses control of the store to the construction people, who have absolutely no concern for customers, employees, or sales. They are there to tear down, build up, and get out. I had a great team of managers who kept their focus on running the store and getting sales. Without them I would have been lost. Ralph, the assistant manager, was very much in his element with construction workers. At six foot four inches tall and a pastime of rebuilding muscle cars, he had some common ground with the construction workers.

The second assistant, Sue, had to overcome some obstacles caused by this male-dominated industry that seldom showed anyone respect, let alone a very pleasant and attractive woman.

She knew she had to pick the right time and place for an eventual showdown. The place was the back room. That was good because I wouldn't have wanted the customers to see what was coming. The issue was a ladder left by a worker that was in our way. Sue asked once and then twice for the worker to move it. The construction worker challenged Sue by his willful inaction. All you can do is rise to the occasion. Sue not only rose to the occasion but so did the ladder. She picked the "friggin" ladder up over her head, marched it out the back door, and sent it sailing into the field behind the store. The worker went to say something, looked at Sue's face, and made the right choice and wisely said, "Sorry."

With my team in place and now back in charge, the remodel progressed. However, it wasn't without many unbelievable events. Everything that could have gone wrong went wrong. The fortitude of the staff was tested almost daily.

Power is essential to run the store. Light, refrigeration, cash registers, and heat are all required to operate the store and all require electricity. Eight times the power was cut off by construction. All unplanned and all with no warning. We got very good at covering the items that required refrigeration, locking the doors and advising the customers to make their way to the checkouts. Our back-up generator, which ensures the cash registers can still operate during a power failure, would only last for a short amount of time. This became very frustrating for the customers, as some were caught in more than one blackout.

The construction workers took out a sprinkler head three times, resulting in a very large amount of water coming in the store along with a bunch of annoyed men and women in heavy jackets and helmets. When the water pressure in your sprinkler system drops drastically, the fire department always shows up. Of course, we allowed them to park their very large trucks right in front of the store. Try explaining to these guys that they're blocking the fire lane! Nothing a couple of dozen donuts can't fix.

Our store was right under the airport flight path. I got very good at identifying the type of planes flying over the store, from a Boeing 767 to an Airbus 330.

My office didn't have an outside window, but for about a week I did have a skylight. Some people would have called it a hole in the roof. I believe I was the only manager who ever had snow falling on his desk.

While they were building the second entranceway, some of the girders holding up the mezzanine level were exposed to the outside. Unfortunately, the crane operator didn't realize this and hit the girder. I haven't been through an actual earthquake, but if furniture sliding around, light fixtures falling from the ceiling, your desk turning into a bobsled is similar, then I've been in the next closest thing.

Sandstorms happened daily, as every time an outside door would open the dust left from the work done the previous night would swirl around like the sands on the Mojave Desert. The old saying, "A smile costs you nothing" was not applicable during this period, as a smile cost you a mouth full of grit!

December came and went but the remodel went on and on. Winter had come to our town and made itself right at home in our store. Because of the new entranceways, most of the front of the store was torn down and large holes to the outside filled the store with Arctic air. At one point I measured the temperature of the express check out. It was -14° C! We had to heat the store with a propane heater that supplied a million BTUs. Not one cashier complained while we were trying to fix the problem.

The five-month remodel was finally complete in a mere eight months. The store was beautiful and surpassed all of our expectations. During that time the store wasn't the only thing that got rebuilt. I saw an assistant manager take charge and lead his workers through the most frustrating times, always seeing the light at the end of the tunnel – no matter how many cave-ins we had to dig ourselves out from. I saw a second assistant gain confidence in her abilities and earn the respect of the people she worked with. I saw a store of two hundred employees not whining or complaining about the conditions. They just simply saw what needed to be done, and did it.

Stores, like ships, are feminine – she's a looker!

Amazingly, while the construction people were building us a better store, we were building ourselves a stronger team. What doesn't kill you makes you stronger. A remodel is similar to a strike; everyone should experience it, but once is enough!

Da Plan Da Plan

Every year we have a ritual that is very dear to the managers. It's an exercise done with passion, frustration, deception, imagination, intimidation, perspiration, and inspiration. Yes, it's time to negotiate our yearly plan. Our plan is the target for our store sales and profit and would be the basis of our yearly bonus. Our industry is very big on bonuses. They could be as much as fifty percent of our annual salary. Get a good bonus and your life significantly changes.

At one district meeting, the Vice President of Retail Operations came to discuss that year's bonus structure. One manager spoke up and expressed his feelings on the subject. "The bonus cheque is similar to the Sasquatch. We hear it's big, but nobody's ever seen one." That manager is no longer with the company. I believe he's using his creative talents writing a book or something.

The plan meeting would involve the district manager giving the store managers their targets. Then, one at a time, we would discuss the reasons why our plan wasn't fair. If you could be persuasive enough and the district manager believed there was justification, he could take some sales or profit off of one store and put it on another. This pitting managers against managers was not pretty but could be very humourous at times. Managers are magicians at making the store money; they could also do very well for themselves.

Over the years each manager seemed to develop their own unique style to get their opinion heard and then accepted. There was the 'tantrum style': a lot of shouting, anger, and tears. This was effective on new district managers, but if you didn't know when to quit, you just embarrassed yourself without any financial remuneration. A slight variation from the tantrum is the 'intimidation style': a lot of shouting, anger, but no tears. Again this was most effective on new DMs. My style was to build a case with facts, present them in an organized fashion (handouts worked well), and then hope for compassion. Apparently, this didn't work on new DMs or old DMs.

We had one manager who I thought of as the Arnold Palmer of the plan meetings. As the bridges at Augusta National golf course play a significant role in the beauty of the course, this 'Master' of the bonus plan used a bridge that added to the beauty of his plan. A bridge near his store was being closed for major repairs. Arnold argued this would impede traffic from getting to his store. That made sense and his plan was lowered. In actuality, the bridge closure trapped the customers and Arnold's store sales went up. He earned one hundred percent bonus. Why is he the 'Master'? Think about it. Due to the bridge closing, he got his plan lowered; Arnold was now in the perfect position to have his plan lowered again because the bridge was now opening! His bonus was one hundred percent two years in a row!

We had another great manager who was more like the Jack Nicklaus of the plan meetings. While Nicklaus had great success at the British Open, this manager's style was similar to the weather at the British Open. Very windy, ever-changing directions, and could create a storm on a moment's notice. I was in this particular meeting and sitting beside a new manager, Greg. I told him to watch Jack and learn. We were going around the table; everyone putting on their show and it became Jack's turn. I whispered to Greg, "Watch this."

Jack looked at his plan and said, "Looks fine, I'm okay with it." Greg looked at me; I looked back at him. "Wait," I said, "he's using the sleeper approach." This method catches everyone off guard. Just as everything is about to end and everyone wants to go home, you go for another round, hopefully getting everyone to agree so they can just get the heck out of the meeting. I watched Jack closely. Something was not right. The meeting came to an end and no move from Jack. It suddenly dawned on me. Just as Jack Nicklaus did his last walk up the eighteenth hole at St. Andrew's, our Jack was doing his last walk through the plan meeting. Jack announced his retirement. The plan was unimportant as he wouldn't be around in a month.

I want to make it very clear that we were compensated very well for the job we did; however, it was the process of setting the targets that we disagreed with.

These meetings were seldom very positive. Most of us left with last year's poor bonus taste still in our mouth and not very confident that we would be savouring a better flavour next year. We often felt these targets were someone's fantasy. The district manager would be like Ricardo Montalbon from *Fantasy Island*. As we were leaving, he would be saying, "Smiles, everyone, smiles."

Was That Kenny Rogers?

I have always loved to play poker. The camaraderie among friends spending time together and the chance of making some money all contributed to my enjoyment of the game. However, there is no doubt in my mind the real reason I play the game — to out think your opponent. I always viewed poker as a game where you didn't always have to have the best cards to win, you just had to make your opponent think you have the best cards.

It was Saturday afternoon at about 1:30. I got a call from a cashier named Shauna. She was nineteen, attractive, and popular with the courtesy clerks. Shauna was a little on the lazy side and had the ability to talk and move her head in that way that shouts 'attitude.' Her history of calling in on the weekends had become legendary. She called to say she was in a car accident in Red Deer, a small city about an hour and a half north of Calgary. I quickly asked, "Are you okay?" "I'm fine." She said, "But I won't be able make it to work at 4:30. Our car isn't drivable." I explained, "We're really going to be busy and we need you." Shauna replied, "I have no way to get to work." What happened next was a reflex reaction, left over from my old poker days. I called her bluff with a bluff of my own. In order for a bluff to work, you need to be quick and confident. Any sign of hesitation will show weakness on your part. "Shauna, we're not very busy right now, so tell you what, I'll come and pick you up!"

I had caught her off guard. In a flustered voice, Shauna replied, "No, we've already got a ride coming." I saw a weakness in her hand. Time to raise. "Have they left already? 'Cause I could call them, tell them to stay home, and I'll come get you." Shauna had barely enough to call that bet. She replied, "No, they left a half hour ago." I did some quick math: distance travelled, speed travelling, and time to change into her uniform. "Shauna, you should be able to make it to the store by 4:30."

At this point she should have folded her hand, but instead tried to make another raise. Shauna countered with, "My friend hit her head and I'm afraid to leave her alone." I raised her back. "I hope she's all right. Who's coming to pick you up?" Now she was acting on sheer reflex.

"Her parents." There's a term in poker used when all the common cards are exposed and your hand can't possibly lose. It's called 'having the nuts.' "If her parents are coming to pick you up, she won't be left alone then. Will she?"

One last desperate effort on Shauna's part: "Well, I can't possibly make it there until 5:30 and I'm off at 8:30. That's only a three-hour shift and by the contract the shortest shift I can work is four hours." This was too easy; time to go 'all in.' I matched that with, "You're absolutely right. We'll extend your shift to 9:30." That was it. Shauna had no choice but to throw in her hand. Dial tone was all I heard.

Shauna showed up to work at 5:30, worked until 8:30, then punched out, leaving her resignation at the front desk. If you're going to gamble, know what's at stake. If you're gambling with your job, you better know whom you're playing against. The price to play the game just may be too expensive. Know when to hold 'em, know when to fold 'em you know the rest.

Two Flew Over the Cuckoo's Nest

When managing a store, most of your time is spent dealing with people: your employees and the customers. Every now and again a manager would be called upon to deal with visitors that were out of the ordinary, often aggressive, with total disregard to your authority, and always with a different agenda. No, not the district manager. Stores were often visited by wildlife of all shapes and sizes.

Depending on a store's location and the number of times the doors are opened, it was quite common to get animals making their way into the store. I have dealt with dogs, cats, rabbits, gophers, and birds. Some other stores have had deer jump through the front windows, along with moose and bears making themselves very comfortable in their parking lot.

This story might qualify for the "Believe It Or Not" category. However, in defense of this manager, we were never given any direction or training on how to get these unwanted visitors out of the store. For the most part it was trial and error. I found it best to leave the door open and the animal would eventually find their way out. All this required was patience, a very rare quality in managers.

In Alberta we have a very common bird called the magpie. This bird is slightly smaller than a crow but larger than a robin and like the cartoon characters Heckle and Jeckle, they are very annoying. Well, this particular day the sun was shining and the birds were singing. As it would happen a single magpie flew into the store, apparently in search of better acoustics. This bird's squawking sounded more like a bad karaoke night at the local pub. The door was left open to allow it to escape, but before it got out another magpie flew in. Now there were two tone deaf 'collaborators' squawking together. Similar to the two friends who just consumed enough courage by the end of the night to perform at the pub and then quickly clear everyone out.

This store manager wasn't what you would call a calm or relaxed sort of a guy. I would more accurately describe him as a 'shoot first, ask questions later' kind of fellow. He was absolutely beside himself trying to get these two birds out of the store. They were flying all over the sales area, probably looking for an escape, but the doors were now closed. This manager wasn't going to take a chance and have another bird fly into the building. The last thing he wanted to do is explain how a 'flock' or 'choir' of birds got into his store.

A few hours went by and a mother and son were at the deli giving an order to the clerk. The boy, about seven years old, was very curious about the birds. He asked the female deli clerk, "Do you know you have birds in the store?" The clerk, weighing their cold cuts, answered the reasonable question. "Why yes, they're our pets." This answer seemed to excite our future 'National Audubon Society' member.' "Do you have names for them?" Our deli clerk was beginning to suspect she may have started something but kept playing along. "No, not yet." Instantly the boy asked to name them. This freckled- faced kid, eyes now sparkling as he pondered the possibilities in his mind. It wasn't long before he declared, "I got it!" Very proudly he announced, "How about Salt and Pepper?" The black and white colouring of the birds must have given him some inspiration. Suddenly, a loud blast echoed through the store, and then another, followed by an eerie, deathly silence.

Oh somewhere in this grocery world the tills are full of cash. The clerks are wheeling groceries out and not a single crash. All the staff was working with the birds that flew about. But there are no birds flying now, Salt and Pepper have checked out.

This soon-to-be former store manager asked his son to come to the store with his 22-calibre rifle and shoot the two birds. This manager was quickly placed in another store, a mall store, with no chance of any air traffic. The meat manager at the new store thought it necessary to post a 'No Hunting' sign in his cutting room. The manager retired soon thereafter. I guess that's one way to end a career in a blaze of glory.

I Hear Bells

Christmas at the store was a very exciting time filled with many contradictions. The additional business was motivating and inspiring. It was very satisfying to see our store's hard work being rewarded in strong sales from our customers. The Christmas week usually generated about thirty percent more sales. We never hired extra staff for the increased sales, as we were able to utilize our part-time staff at full-time hours and our full-time staff at overtime. This was good for all concerned. We didn't have to deal with inexperienced employees during such a significant time, and the staff earned extra money that helped to minimize the added expenses during the festive season.

Now with the extra business and longer hours at work tiring you out, you also had the burden of Christmas shopping, entertaining, and being entertained. I always found being entertained took the most out of me. It's amazing how Christmas carols can get you all revved up, at the same time you're dragging your feet because the night before you did your infamous impression of Santa's reindeer crash landing during the store's Christmas Party. The staff and customers were pushed to their limits, but somehow they all kept it together. I know its cliché to say, but there is a magic that does affect the human spirit during this time of year.

We would always put together a staff luncheon at the store, usually the final Saturday before Christmas Day. I felt it was very important for me to get personally involved. I wanted the staff to know just how much I appreciated their hard work. So I took the glory job of cooking the turkeys. Actually, I had help from one of our cake decorators, Jelica. She was from Croatia and was an excellent cook. I couldn't help but challenge her to a turkey cook off. We prepared and cooked two large turkeys each. My plan was to cook a less traditional bird while she cooked the conventional style birds, with stuffing, sage, and poultry seasoning.

I chose a path less travelled. I started mine the day before, by giving the two turkeys a light rub down with olive oil, followed by a deep workout with liquid smoke (hickory), then let them sit overnight.

In the morning, I cut up lemons, limes and oranges and stuffed my thirsty birds till they couldn't hold any more citrus. A generous sprinkling of Mrs. Dash and Hi's seasoning salt, and the birds were ready for their bath. I smuggled a couple of beers into the store to put in the pan with some water. We had the pizza ovens in the store to cook the turkeys. Lots of basting and five hours later, you have "Dave's Twang Tang Turkey."

The entire meal was a team effort. Other staff would help by cooking the potatoes, beans, and gravy, making the salads, and decorating the coffee room. It really was a large production that couldn't be done by just a few people. We would serve about a hundred and twenty employees during that afternoon.

Every year as a store, we adopted a struggling family to provide a Christmas meal and presents for Christmas morning. We had an idea one year to charge the staff two dollars for our meal and the money we collected would go towards the adopted family. It sounded like a good idea to me and the department managers agreed. A sign was posted, an announcement made, and a jar was put in the coffee room. We were good to go.

Irene Crasler

The Christmas birds, Jelica, and one turkey

I was in the coffee room serving turkey (make that campaigning for my bird) and I noticed one of the meat wrappers, Jane, being very upset about the two-dollar charge. Some of the other employees tried to defend it, but this just made her angrier and louder. I invited her into the boardroom. If there's one thing I learned from dealing with upset customers, it's never give them an audience other than you. Jane reluctantly came into the room and sat down. I closed the door and made sure I sat down beside her and not across from her. My purpose wasn't to challenge her or confront her; I just wanted to understand. "Jane, what was that all about?" I asked in my most humble manner. She was very upset but was able to tell me her thoughts. "This is our Christmas lunch, a gift from you and the company to us, the employees. This is a hard company to work for; they expect a lot out of us. This was the one time of the year that I felt they thanked us. And now we have to pay two dollars to be thanked!

Her puffy eyes were about to leak a little fluid. I felt like I had just watched the sad part of *It's a Wonderful Life*. Jane was absolutely right. "I don't know what to say, but I am sorry. You're right. I'll take the sign down and explain to everyone that it was wrong, I made a mistake."

Jane suggested that we keep the jar up so if anyone wants to donate, they can. I always said, "As a manager, you don't have to come up with the good ideas, just recognize them."

I still felt that there was more to the story. Jane was still upset. I gently prodded a little deeper. Jane, was reluctant at first to share some of her past, but gradually it started coming, then a little more and then look out, I needed Dr. Phil! She explained that her family had been adopted each Christmas, but her Christmas would get returned to the store so her mom could buy cigarettes and spirits. This lady had a tough life but had worked very hard to find her way. It wasn't easy but she did it. We shared a thank you hug; her thanking me for listening and me thanking her for enlightening me.

Later that day, Jane was up enjoying the lunch (she chose Jelica's turkey). On her way out, she very quietly went by the donation jar and slid a ten-dollar bill into it. I couldn't help but think; "Every time a bell rings an angel gets his wings." Sometimes that bell only rings inside you, but your wings are earned nevertheless.

Five Letter Word for Terminated

After thirty years in the retail grocery industry — most of these years being spent on the front line in the stores — the company saw an opportunity for me to be utilized in a different role. I was offered a position in the Labour Relations department, as an advisor. This job was to act as a resource for the stores, plants or warehouses, involving interpretation or disputes over the contract. To be successful in this department one required an open mind, empathy, clear and precise communication skills, an ability to get two parties to come to a resolve, and have all involved feel like they were victorious. Simple.

I really enjoyed this job. I was able to work with about eighty stores and countless Union business agents. I wasn't trained for this job, so that posed a few problems. At the beginning, my experience served me well, but it left many preconceived viewpoints. I was informed that my early investigations were done from a "hawkish" vantagepoint. Meaning I had formed an opinion before the investigation was over, thus tainting much of the information collected. It was hard to stay unbiased, when many of the employees we were dealing with I knew from my past. It seemed that twenty percent of the employees created eighty percent of the disciplines. However, to be fair, twenty percent of the managers tended to generate eighty percent of the grievances. Grievances occurred when neither side could agree on a resolution in the store, that being the store manager and usually the business agent (a representative of the union actually employed by the union).

These committed union individuals were relentless in their fight for justice. If they felt that the huge, impersonal, multi-national corporation was unfairly treating a helpless employee, they were on us like salt on a peanut. I was often reminded of the Tasmanian devil character. The frustrating part for us was that a lot of their efforts went to protecting employees who were guilty. The agents had very little choice; they were there to represent the employee, regardless of guilt or innocence. This often left the agents or their lawyers in many less than desirable situations.

We had an arbitration involving a workplace violence issue in our ice cream plant. Allegedly, two women got into an altercation in the coffee room and the company terminated the one we found to be the instigator. I had been visualizing two very heavy older women to be involved. When I got to the arbitration room and saw the two very attractive eighteen-year-old girls involved, I thought to myself, "The Amazon Warriors at the Willie Wonka Chocolate Factory."

I felt bad for the union lawyer because he was struggling with the case. We had several witnesses that supported the action we took. Our primary witness was in the coffee room and saw the entire melee. When cross-examining our witness, this lawyer tried to downplay the fight. "Wouldn't it be more accurate to say it wasn't really a punch, but more of an open-handed slap?" the union lawyer suggested. The young witness shook her head and said, "No." The lawyer continued. "And wouldn't it be even more accurate to say that it wasn't even a slap, but more like a push to the shoulder?" The lawyer demonstrated with a very light motion. The witness, now very frustrated, stood up and said, "Absolutely not!" The witness clenched her left hand as if she was grabbing a handful of hair. The witness continued, "She grabbed the back of this girl's head," now the witness formed a fist with her right hand, "and then she punched her five times as hard as she could!" The witness now mimicked the punches while counting out, "one, two, three, four, five!"

The union lawyer took a step back, surprised at the veracity of the witness. After a brief pause to collect his thoughts, he announced, "I object, Mr. Arbitrator. The witness has no idea how hard this girl can punch." Our lawyer calmly stood up and volunteered, "We'll accept just hard." He sat down, trying to suppress his delight with the cross-examination. The arbitrator supported the action the company took.

We had terminated two employees for "sweet-hearting." This is when one person sells product to another person at an extremely discounted price. The product in question was a case of cleaning solution that should have sold for $40.00. The department manager instead sold it to a clerk in the store for $8.00. Two movie tapes were sold for $5.00 each that should have retailed for $20.00 each.

This was captured on video, the cash register transaction was found and the two admitted they did it. Somehow they felt they weren't guilty and shouldn't have been terminated.

We went to arbitration. These two individuals cost the union a huge expense in lawyer fees and many hours of the business agent's time assisting in creating a defence. Then double that when you realize the company has to spend a similar amount to present our case. Then add the cost and time of the arbitrator, witnesses, and the expense of the room. This whole process was ridiculous.

While the department manager was on the stand, her story started changing from the original. While this was happening, both our lawyer and myself noticed that the clerk wasn't paying any attention to the new story his accomplice was creating. Instead, he was immersed in a newspaper. On our break I walked past the clerk and noticed that he was diligently working on a crossword puzzle! When he went on the stand, he told the old version of the story. Their defence quickly unravelled. I looked across the room at the department manager, and she was now looking at the same paper. I thought to myself, "Unbelievable." As we finished up and were leaving the room, I looked to see if she had finished the crossword puzzle. What I saw was the paper not opened to the puzzle, instead it was opened to the Help Wanted section. Apparently the department manager *was* paying attention. Both terminations were upheld.

Family Affair

Each store has a position that acts as the glue that keeps the team together. They seem to know every customer and their relatives, all the employees, and their next door neighbours. Most of the time they were the ones organizing the Christmas parties and the staff barbecues. If you were curious as to who was dating whom in the store or who was fighting with whom, these people somehow always knew. They're in tune with what's happening and very often give guidance to the managers. I found these people to be excellent sounding boards, as they were often better connected to the staff and often had opposing opinions, which would give me a greater viewpoint. The position that was unofficially responsible for all this extra effort was the head teller.

The head teller was responsible for the front end running smoothly. They oversaw the cashiers and the courtesy clerks, wrote schedules for both, evaluated both groups, and were responsible for balancing the books. Now that I think about it, they didn't leave much for the manager to do!

Now I cannot tell you how this person gained these extraordinary qualities. Whether through genealogy, similar to how salmon instinctively know what river to swim up to find their spawning grounds, or a secret society similar to the mason's that passed this information down to its members, I don't know. Perhaps we'll never know and that may not be a bad thing. Sometimes too many questions and too much information could prove to be dangerous. I simply accepted it and put my trust in these people.

After being full-time for a while, it was time for me to assume greater responsibilities. One evening each week, I was put in charge of the store. This included directing the work force, handling customer complaints, and if it got busy to help in the office approving cheques. Now there was no debit card in those days and we didn't accept credit cards.

This meant that the only way to pay for groceries was by cash or cheque. Seventy percent of the sales were paid for by cheque. In order for me to be effective in this role, I required extensive training. There were many steps to properly approve a cheque:

- Trust no one
- Ask for two pieces of ID, one with a picture
- Address on cheque must match address on ID
- Date must be correct, double check the year if it's January
- Body and figure must match
- Cheque must be signed
- Search the stop list file for previous NSF cheques
- While checking the stop list give them the 'look' that makes them all feel guilty they're paying by cheque instead of cash.

I had the standard one-minute explanation of these rules and was sent out to the trenches. I was a little uncomfortable with this part of the job, but seldom got in a situation that required me to approve cheques. Of course, the first night I was in charge it got busy and I had to send the office person (the cashier responsible for cheque approval) to cash and I took over the office. I was immediately required to approve a cheque. I know I was nervous and it showed but I persevered. I went through the rules as I was taught and approved my first cheque. It wasn't so tough. I actually felt proud of myself. Until the next day. I was called to the office and the manager and head teller, Marie, were standing together. That's what they'd do, they would stand together and point out my mistakes. I could see it was going to be a tag team match, and me without a partner.

The manager was holding the first cheque I approved. "Did you approve this?" the store manager asked in a very interrogative manner. I looked at the cheque, saw my initials on the back and admitted, "Yes." My manager said, "What were you thinking?" Marie's head was shaking in disapproval. In defence I stated, "I got all the information required." "Did you read the address?" the manager inquired. "The address matched the ID," I quickly replied. The manager agreed it did. "My friend, if this cheque bounces, you'll have one hell of a drive to collect payment!" I looked at the address and thought to myself, just how far is Yellowknife?

It's against company policy." The lady quickly turned from a pleasant tone to a little annoyed. "It's okay, Marie does it for me all the time." I quickly recalled rule number one (trust no one). Again I said I was sorry but Marie was not in, so again I stated I couldn't do it. The daughter now got into the act and said, "Do you think my mother is lying?" I held back my first thought and offered to call Marie at home. This seemed to calm the situation down, but not for long. There was no answer at Marie's house, most likely bingo night. Again, I said, "Sorry," but now the lady in the wheelchair got belligerent.

I've been called names before: "Asshole," "Bastard," "Prick" and many more, but nothing ever stung as much as the label this lady put on me. "You're nothing but a stupid bimbo!" That hurt. I can live with stupid but using a feminine context like "Bimbo"? That was a personal attack on my manhood! I asked them to leave in my most masculine voice, and not so politely.

The next day I was sharing that story with Marie when the phone rang. Marie picked it up and of course it was that irate lady with the wheelchair. Marie listened for a brief moment then said, "Stop it right there! If I ever hear you treating an employee like that again, you'll have me to deal with, and believe me it won't be pretty!" Marie added, "This is my family here. You attack them, you attack me." At that point I think I was cheering, at least on the inside. Marie continued, "Now I suggest if you want your cheque cashed, you wheel your butt down here — minus the attitude!"

After that incident, I realized we were family. It's okay for family to give you a hard time, but if it's anyone else you better be prepared to take on the whole store.

And The Winner Is!

Have you ever entered a contest in a store and wondered, "Just how honest is the draw going to be?" This story should answer that question. I was very proud of our company's, our store's, our employees' and our customer's willingness to help out people less fortunate than us. This would be shown by donations made, causes backed, emergency relief provided, and so forth. Each store also allowed the employees to pick a charity and everyone would raise money throughout the year. We had an on-going book sale, we sold candies, and had special promotions the company put on that encouraged both donations and sales.

Our store decided to buy a fifty-inch Panasonic rear projection TV. It regularly sold for $2000.00, but one of our employees was able to negotiate an even better price of $1800.00. We displayed this magnificent piece of technology at the front of the store and printed up four thousand tickets to sell. They sold like wildfire. I heard one customer say, "I have a dream, a dream that one day my children won't judge a TV by the quality of its colour, but rather by the quality of its content." I replied, "Until that day (and I'm doubtful it will ever happen) you better try to win that TV!"

The plan was to sell the four thousand tickets and have the draw at the local pub by the store where we were having the final wind-up party. The pub helped out by giving our charity a dollar for every jug of beer sold that night and a dime for every chicken wing eaten. I don't think it gets much better than that. Drink and eat, and all the time you're earning money for a worthy cause. Tough job but somebody has to do it! We hired a singer for the night, and he, along with the pub employees, helped to sell the remaining tickets to the patrons.

It was a very successful evening. Everyone enjoyed him or herself, lots of tickets were sold and money raised. We brought the thirty-seven hundred tickets that we had already sold and then sold the remaining three hundred tickets at the bar.

As the evening was winding down, we had the singer draw the name for the fifty-inch rear projection Panasonic TV. Our luck continued as the winner of the TV was there at the bar as we announced the name.

Even better luck, he had a truck and we were able to load the prize onto the back of the truck and it was out of our hands in less than an hour. I left that night feeling pretty good about our store and the volunteers that put this event together.

I was at the store the next day still feeling proud of the previous night's events. About 11:00 am, a familiar face poked his head in my office. It was the bartender from the previous night. Funny, but I immediately noticed that they don't look so cheery when they're not serving you a drink. "Hey, how are you?" I said. "Great job last night." The bartender had a concerned look on his face and a box in his hand. "I found this box under the bar this morning," he informed me. I looked in the box and a sudden feeling of panic came over me. I was looking at approximately thirty-seven hundred TV draw tickets. The bartender added, "These tickets never got into the draw." What I suspected, but not what I wanted to hear. The tickets we had previously sold didn't get put into the barrel with the tickets we sold that night. I was silent for a moment then blurted out, "Does anyone know about this?" The bewildered bartender said "No." I quickly pondered the possibility of just letting it be. Unfortunately, I have that little voice that would nag me till I did the right thing.

I informed my boss and the public affairs person of our blunder. Not surprising, the first question they asked me was "Does anyone else know about this?" Apparently, they both have the same little voice that I do, as it wasn't long before they agreed to my plan.

I called up the gentleman who won the TV. The first thing I said was, "I just want to congratulate you on the win. I want you to understand that you won it and it's your TV, but I also want you to understand how you won it." I explained about the mix up, and as I was talking I could hear the TV in the background with his children screaming and laughing. I thought to myself, "Not good." I continued and explained that the TV retailed for $2,000.00 dollars.

I reminded him of our charity and that this slip up will cost the charity money. I proposed that we give him $1,000.00 to get the TV back and put his entry back into the draw. Our winner mulled it over that evening. The next morning he answered with "Sorry buddy, I'm keeping the TV."

Time for plan B. We talked to the supplier of the TV and they sold us another one and took $200.00 off the $1,800.00 original price.

Our Public Affairs Department gave us $800.00 to split the cost. We were able to minimize the loss and gained a huge lesson about responsibility and integrity. So if you ever wonder, "Are those contests fixed?" Trust me, they're honest, and sometimes you may even get a better chance than originally advertised.

A Grocery Story

In other stories I've said that Christmas in retail can be the most frustrating time of the year and the most heart-warming. Just when you think you're going to drown in a sea of eggnog, a little Christmas magic always seem to appear and one of Santa's helpers throws you a lifesaver.

I had a rule that I would be the last person to leave the store every Christmas Eve. I'm not positive why I made that rule for myself, whether it was so I could be sure everything was left reasonable, or to ensure that we closed at the time we advertised. Almost every Christmas Eve, our large clock that was prominent on the sales floor seemed to run a little fast. I could always find a broom near-by that could just reach the arms on the clock, so that I could reset the correct time.

Another possible reason I stayed could be best described using a golf training term: 'muscle memory.' That's when a motion, usually your swing, becomes natural because of repetition. In the old days, before I became a manager, it was quite common to have a sip or two of the 'Old Christmas spirit.' Okay, I'll admit it; it was usually the best back room party of the year. I swear that one Christmas Eve, I drove up to a red light beside Santa, along with Dasher, Dancer, and the rest of the boys. Turned out it was a Coca Cola truck, in Christmas theme. As manager, however, I wouldn't be staying to partake in one of these parties, but to prevent them. These days you could lose your job for celebrating during your shift.

I suppose the real reason I stayed was because I needed to be there at the toughest time of the year. I always believed that I couldn't ask someone to do something that I would not do myself. It also provided an opportunity to make some small Christmas magic happen, whether it was finding that item that no one else could locate or sneaking a customer in the store after we closed so they could get that cranberry jelly they forgot. Another Christmas saved.

It was also a privilege to wish everyone a Merry Christmas as they left work to start their holiday. It always felt more than that of an employer to an employee; it was friends wishing friends a Merry Christmas.

Christmas Day was another story. We had to check the store some time during the day to ensure it was secure and that all the refrigeration was working. One compressor going down could cost the company tens of thousands of dollars. I usually checked the store about noon; that would allow me to be at my parents' by two and partake in the open house they always had.

These gatherings had become legendary over the years, and there was no way I would miss it. My family, aunts, uncles, cousins, and friends would find their way to my parents' house. Once there, they were treated to sausage rolls, bacon-wrapped scallops, short bread cookies, and if you were really good that year you might be able to talk my dad into making his 'mind numbing' martinis. (Dad says the secret is to shake the martini in the shaker twenty-one times. No more, no less.) All I know is whatever the ingredients or chemistry my parents used to create the magic around this party made it my favourite part of Christmas.

This one particular Christmas Day, I got to my store at just after twelve. I was always astounded at the number of cars driving by to see if we were open. The drive-by was always accompanied by the constant ringing of the phone by customers calling to see if we were open. I'm sure I was witnessing a little foreshadowing of the future; one day we would be open. However, that day we were closed and all I wanted to do was get out of the store and get to my parents'. Being in a closed grocery isn't what you think. The first thing you notice is all the smells in the store. Not always good smells; when a store is closed it quickly goes stale; no inviting fragrances coming from the bakery, that's for certain. The store is always dark; the one day the store gets to sleep. However, it doesn't sleep soundly, as the noises of the store can be creepy. Pipes contracting, engines starting, and air blowing all make for a barrage of pings, pangs, and pops. If you weren't familiar with the sound track, it could be a tad unnerving.

I had to walk through the store and test the temperature of every refrigerated unit. I had my path planned out, temperature gun in one hand, and to get me through the next twenty minutes, some wine gums in the other hand. I started in the deli and worked my way around the perimeter of the store. So far, so good. Now for the middle of the store, that would be the dairy and frozen sections.

I was looking down the freezer aisle and saw my greatest fear. A puddle of water. This was a sure indication that the refrigeration unit wasn't working. I looked again. The sun was glaring in the wax, making it difficult to see, but nevertheless, there it was, a puddle of water, smack in the middle of the aisle. Now I thought to myself, did I really see that or was it part of the glare? If my vision was true, I'd have to pull out the entire contents of the freezer that was defrosting. It would take about one hundred fifty milk trays to pull the section and save the product from spoiling. That would take three to four hours. I'd miss the open house! I thought about it, but again that little voice inside me kept nagging and I knew what I had to do.

I called my parents and explained the situation to my mom. "Can't you call someone to come and help you?" she suggested. I explained, "I can't call someone in on Christmas. I'll just do it myself." Using my most hard done by voice, I added, "I should be able to make it for dinner."

Christmas magic always seems to happen when you least expect it, or when you've already resigned yourself to accept a less than desirable outcome. About a half-hour after I hung up the phone, I heard the sound of keys tapping on the window at the front of the store. With the sun at his back, I could just make out my dad's silhouette. With Mom holding down the fort, Dad came across town to help me pull the downed freezer. What should have taken me four hours only took my dad and me about an hour and a half.

My Christmas was not only saved but also enriched by the selfless efforts of my parents. I don't remember the gift I got under the tree that year, but the gift I got that afternoon, I'll remember forever.

Express Checkout
Nine Sentences or Less

There was a buggy full of banana squash sitting in the back room. A clerk decided to wheel it out on to the sales floor. He put a sign on it and walked away. We assumed it was a price sign. After many confused and curious faces and one possible coronary from customers reading the sign, I thought I should investigate. The sign stated, "Batteries not included!"

◊ ◊ ◊

A customer at the check stand decided that the watermelon she chose wasn't big enough. A clerk volunteered to get her a bigger one. His first attempt was met with, "No, that's still not big enough." His second and third attempts were met with a similar response. On his fourth attempt, the frustrated clerk simply threw a package of watermelon seeds onto the check stand and said, "Here, grow your own!"

◊ ◊ ◊

When confronting a shoplifter who had taken ten packages of shrimp and stuffed them in his blue backpack, I was embarrassed to find nothing in the pack. He had dumped the shrimp down an aisle when we lost sight of him. I had no choice but to let him and his backpack leave the store. I followed him out and watched him until he left the parking lot. As I re-entered the store, I noticed a display of blue backpacks.

◊ ◊ ◊

When courtesy clerks select a check stand to wrap groceries at, it's a good bet that the cutest and most available cashier will require the help. At a cashier meeting, one frustrated cashier stood up and asked, "What do I have to do to get a wrapper around here, get a divorce?"

Today, customers' expectations are so high: "They want their cake and eat it too, and now lose weight at the same time."

◊ ◊ ◊

I had just got my first store as manager. On my second Sunday, I got a call from a friend who was in charge for the day of my old store. "Dave, we haven't had a bank pick up since Wednesday: I have $750,000 in cash at the store. What should I do?" I replied, "Get a brown paper bag and meet me in the parking lot!"

◊ ◊ ◊

A few years ago, we were downsizing the company. A very sharp manager said: "We are FRIED! Forced Retirement In Every Department."

◊ ◊ ◊

I received a phone call from our employment representative. She asked me about an employee in the store who was applying for a job at our head office. I informed her he was a pretty good worker. The employment rep then asked if there was anything else I would like to add. I asked her if she had a hammer. "What in the world would I need a hammer for?" I answered, "You'll need to nail everything down if you don't want him to steal it." This employee was applying for a job in the office, while currently suspended and subsequently terminated for theft!

◊ ◊ ◊

A produce clerk was terminated for theft on a Thursday. He had been helping himself to free groceries at the end of his shifts. That Saturday night, he and his wife showed up at the produce manager's door to attend the Department's Christmas party. Sort of reminds me of the Christmas Eve during World War I when the British and German soldiers ceased firing to sing carols together.

A customer in an Edmonton store was looking for crab apples. Apparently she had a recipe for a crab apple pie handed down to her from her grandmother, who just happened to be visiting later that week. Crab apples are not a commercial apple and I don't honestly recall ever having them available. The lady was visibly disappointed. The produce clerk asked the customer if she could come back in about an hour. On his lunch break, this clerk drove home, jumped his fence, and proceeded to pick two bags of crab apples from his neighbour's tree. Truly a great service story.

◊ ◊ ◊

The first snowstorm of the year always provided a little entertainment for the veteran clerks. Like clockwork, you could always count on a new hire asking for the "winter tires" to put on the shopping carts!

◊ ◊ ◊

Our president was discussing the importance of service to a group of managers. He told us of a customer in California that was returning a sponge. Apparently, this sponge, when left in the kitchen, could somehow make its way to the top of the TV in the living room. When locked in the closet to prevent it from wandering, the constant pounding on the door would keep this customer awake all night. Our president said, "Without question, we refunded the money." On a side note, he added with a mischievous grin, "I would have loved to been able to take the sponge, race back to the customer's house, and leave the sponge leaning against his front door."

◊ ◊ ◊

There were always customers who stood out from the crowd. I found value in taking the time to talk to them and share stories. One special guy was a seventy-six year-old gentleman, who would sit on a bench we had at the front of the store while his daughter shopped. Once we were discussing my bungie jumping experience. The gentleman said, "You'd never get me to do that," but he did say he enjoyed hang gliding. At that time, hang gliding might have been popular for about twenty years. I was impressed; he must have been one of the pioneers of the sport and I told him so. Very modestly he said, "I don't think so, I only started gliding last year!"

I was the first assistant at a store that, at the time, had the largest volume in Canada. We had a customer slip and fall in an aisle near the back of the store, and he couldn't get up. I made the decision to call 911 and get an ambulance. I was waiting outside in front of the doors to guide the paramedics to the fallen customer. They soon arrived and as I was taking them to the fallen customer, another customer fainted at a check stand. The paramedics stopped to assist her. I was informed they are to assist the first victim they find. I was forced to call another ambulance. The 911 operator asked, "Have you got a war going on over there?" I very casually replied, "No, it's just Saturday."

◊ ◊ ◊

I had just been transferred to an older store in an established area of town. I was excited about the store, but it did have one area of huge concern -- graffiti. It was mean-spirited, very personal stuff about staff in the store, and it was everywhere. This had to stop and had to stop now. After careful consideration and surveying the resources on hand, I selected the second man in Produce to take the role of "graffiti remover." This gentleman didn't do it, but as I informed him that that didn't matter; any graffiti, anywhere, and Don had to clean it up. I explained that if he wanted to express his feelings to the rest of the staff that would be all right. He did and the graffiti immediately stopped. As I had always believed, you must have the right person for the right job. Don was six foot nine and weighed well over three hundred pounds!

◊ ◊ ◊

This story made it across North America; the Associated Press picked it up. We used to be closed four days a year: Christmas Day, Boxing Day, New Year's Day, and Easter Sunday. One Easter Sunday the Calgary Police Services got a call that they should investigate this particular store. When they arrived, they found several customers going through the check stands paying for their groceries. This wouldn't be unusual except the store was closed and there was not one employee in the store. A door was left unlocked and the customers took the initiative to help themselves, including paying for their items. It was believed not one item went out that wasn't paid for. Thank you, Calgary!

It was April Fool's Day and a clerk in one of the stores played one of the oldest tricks in the book: he inked the black phone receiver with black ink. I'm not a fan of this trick but the deed was done; the manager had ink all over his face. No one in the store was going to tell him, possibly because of that old adage, "Don't shoot the messenger." Later on that day, the district manager came into the store, saw the ink, and said nothing about it. "I'll do a quick tour of the store and make one quick phone call and I'll be out of here." The tour was done, the phone call made, and with the identical outcome. Now visualize the two of them, staring at the ink on each other's face, and not one of them said a word. I can only imagine what was said at home.

◊ ◊ ◊

Sometimes you can't help but cry over spilt milk. A courtesy clerk carelessly packed a four-litre jug of one percent milk in the trunk of a customer's new Saturn. The jug broke and emptied its entire contents into the back seat of the car. The lady brought the car back to the store for a closer examination. It was January and cold. When I saw the car, I apologized and had her go to a detailing shop. She brought the bill back and we paid just under $100.00. The next time I saw this lady was the first hot day in spring. She asked me to smell her car and, my God, it was ripe! Apparently the only way to get rid of the sour milk smell was to replace the interior...only $1,800.00!

◊ ◊ ◊

Halloween always provided a special challenge to retailers. So why wouldn't we sell five flats of eggs (one hundred fifty eggs) at 8:00 pm on Halloween night to two sixteen-year-old boys? I always believed the store had a responsibility to the community and to sell these eggs would be irresponsible. I informed the young men that I couldn't sell them the eggs as I believed they were not going to be used as originally intended. They assured me they were for a restaurant in Cochrane, a small town just west of Calgary. I made a deal with them. "If you give me the number of the restaurant and they confirm you are purchasing these eggs on their behalf, I'll give the eggs to you for free. Deal or no deal?" No deal. They left the store without the eggs and us without egg on our face.

As a service initiative, we were required to thank customers by their last names when the opportunity was presented. Many employees had difficulties pronouncing the last names and felt the first name was okay. I would tell these struggling employees about a scene I witnessed in a Red Deer store. A young husband and wife were just finishing going through a checkout, in which the husband paid the very attractive female cashier with his credit card and club card. The cashier read his name but couldn't pronounce his last name and elected the easy way out. "Thank you, John, we'll see you again." John was a little surprised at the familiarity, but his wife's face told another story. As the couple was walking away from the check stand, the wife, in a very distrusting tone, said, "Who's that?" The husband very innocently answered, "I don't know." As the wife hastened her walk, she disgustedly replied, "Yeah, right!"

◊ ◊ ◊

Tuesdays are new DVD release days. The bigger the movie, the bigger the buzz around the release. Finding Nemo was being released this particular Tuesday. The problem was I was finding Nemo in people's jackets, under their sweaters, and I stopped one gentleman with twenty-five copies in his backpack. I didn't have the time it takes to deal with processing a shoplifter, so I took the DVDs back and told the shoplifter not to come back. He agreed and then asked for his backpack. I thought about it for a while, then told him no, as he would just use it to steal from someone else and if he had a problem with that, to call the cops. The backpack was blue!

◊ ◊ ◊

Every Saturday night after the store closes, we used to remove all the fresh bread, because it would be outdated when we reopened Monday morning. I was in the freezer aisle when I found a newly promoted clerk and asked him to take the bread, put an X on each package with a black marker, and stack them in a basket to sell Monday at ten for a dollar. I assumed he understood, but you know what they say when you assume -- something about making an ass of you and me. I came to work Monday morning to find a basket in the freezer aisle loaded with what used to be frozen bread dough. The packages had exploded through the plastic bag and were oozing through the wire frame of the basket and onto the floor. I realized then that, I had been standing beside the display area of the frozen bread dough when I explained to the clerk what to do. Honestly, between you and me, this guy was not the sharpest tool in the shed.

◊ ◊ ◊

In every large corporation, the most difficult area to excel in is communication. We were instructed to put candy sprinkles on half of our donuts. Each donut was to have sprinkles on one half and icing on the other half. I suggested to my DM, what they meant was to put sprinkles on fifty percent of the donuts made, not on fifty percent of every donut made! "Can't you follow simple instructions?" was his reply to my questioning attitude. We did as we were told. A few months later a representative from the office that issued the instructions came to my store, saw the donuts, and had only one question. "Can't you follow simple instructions?"

◊ ◊ ◊

I was at the customer service desk when a large man in his fifties slammed down a package of fresh pork chops on the counter. "These are the worst pork chops I have ever seen," he said. I came back with, "Yes, they do look like horrible chops." I had caught the customer off guard. He countered with, "Can't you back your product better than that?" "Certainly we back our product better than that. It's the competitor's product we have trouble with!" I had noticed our competitor's label on the product. "I'm sorry, I made a mistake," he said, ready to take the chops back. I said, "You made a mistake going there in the first place. We'll replace them for you here." Never give a competitor a chance to make things right. For $7.50 we just made a customer for life.

It was a very hot and sunny July afternoon and I was having a beer at one of the many outdoor beer gardens that the world famous Calgary Stampede has to offer. Stampede, like Christmas, only comes once a year, so everyone makes the most of it, kicking up their heels and letting their hair down. While I was sitting down surveying all the sights the Stampede can provide, I noticed a very attractive lady giving me a very long look! She was sitting alone so I did the neighbourly thing and flashed her my best "How you doing?" smile. She countered with an "I'm doing fine" smile of her own. Just as I was running the rest of the evening through my mind, a very large gentleman sat down beside her, bringing with him two beers. At that moment the lady with the long stare and beautiful smile announced, in what she thought was a whisper, "Honey, look, it's our Safeway store manager! I didn't know they're allowed to drink!" I quickly got another beer and began to run the rest of the evening through my mind.

◊ ◊ ◊

I was fortunate in my career to be the manager of a brand new store; involved from the planning stages, through construction, and set up. The opening was a gala event, filled with lots of pomp and circumstance, where we were spoiled with the amount of help we could utilize. We hired four people for two weeks and the only job they had was to sign up people for our cheque-cashing card. My mom was one of the people we hired (what goes around, comes around). Actually, my mom did an outstanding job but an opportunity like this seldom comes in any lifetime. With one hour left on her final shift, I called her to my office. She had to walk through a gauntlet of employees with heads bowed, and all aware of what was coming. In my best Donald Trump impression, I looked at my mom and said, "You're fired!" My mom had a puzzled look, but quickly realized she could still send me to my room! Not wanting to risk finding out who has the power, the manager or the mother, I took it back, allowing her to retire with dignity, minus the retirement party.

I once worked for a district manager who would only accept written communications from the managers in blue ink. If it was black ink it would be sent back. If he couldn't read your signature it would be sent back. That one always puzzled me; if he couldn't read the signature, how did he know who to send it back to?

◊ ◊ ◊

I was an assistant manager eagerly working to become a store manager. My district manager, during a visit, explained what was required to get a promotion. "First," he said, "you don't wear your sports jacket enough on the sales floor." "Second, you let your hair get a little long." Then with a little uneasiness, he said, "And last, about your moustache, it's been discussed at the office. Some people, not me mind you, don't like it." I couldn't believe what I was hearing. I thanked the DM for his suggestions and went on about my business, contemplating the information I was just given. It then dawned on me. He wasn't telling me how to be a better manager, he was telling me how to get promoted -- two entirely different items. The next week, with sport jacket on, hair cut short and moustache cut off, I was promoted to my first store.

◊ ◊ ◊

We had a slow pitch league in which all the stores participated. My new store that I managed and my old store where I had been the assistant had a game postponed due to rain. I thought it would be fun to challenge my old store to a tournament style game with trophies, a barbecue, and dance afterwards. A date was set, the trophies purchased, and the steaks marinating. Our store of thirty-eight employees fielded a decent team, but as I suspected, we were no match for the old store that chose their team out of a staff of three hundred fifty. At the party, we awarded the trophies to the teams. First place was a beautiful monument that stood about a foot tall. Their captain, Ken, held the winning prize proudly until he saw the second place trophy being awarded; it stood two and a half feet tall and required three players to parade it around the room. Proving once again, size is important and who is assigned the task of purchasing the trophies even more important!

The grocery industry always posed an obstacle when it came to having fun with the rest of the world. Sporting events, long weekends, concerts' and holidays always happened when we seemed to be required at the store. Y2K, the turn of a new millennium, instead of providing an opportunity to celebrate, created a level of concern unlike we had ever experienced. The store managers were instructed to be at their store before midnight and remain there until after one o'clock. The fear was power would be cut, security systems would fail, and computers would freeze up. So much for the biggest party in one thousand years. As it turned out, the fears were all without merit, including missing the best party in a thousand years. Some very special friends, Scott and Shelley, held a New Year's Eve party for a few of us poor and party-less managers. It started at 2:00 am and we celebrated the best New Year's at 4:00 am. These friends saw a potentially disappointing evening and because they possess empathy and imagination, provided an evening that we will all be forever grateful for.

◊ ◊ ◊

Quite often you get a customer experiencing a little financial difficulty. They would ask if they could pay with a post-dated cheque. This is absolutely not allowed. However, once in a while someone with a sincere look could get me to take the post-dated cheque and I would give him or her cash to pay for their groceries. One time I did this and lost the twenty-five dollar cheque the lady gave me, but I didn't think much of it. Six months later this lady's husband reminded me that the cheque had not been cashed and gave me twenty-five dollars cash -- one ten, two fives, one toonie, and three loonies. Again my faith in mankind was validated.

◊ ◊ ◊

In the grocery industry you seldom got to eat dinner before 7:00 pm. When coming home I would often pick up dinner at a Kentucky Fried Chicken near my place. One evening I was entering the outlet and a cute girl behind the counter smiled at me and whispered to her co-worker. Now I had noticed this girl before, but I didn't realize that she noticed me. I walked up to the counter and said, "Hi, I'll have a five-piece chicken dinner and a small gravy." This girl seemed very excited about my order and turned to her co-worker and said, "See, I told you he would order that!" Some things are good to be recognized for; this was not one of them. I stopped going there after that.

◊ ◊ ◊

I can't describe the respect I gained for Murray when he and I were assigned to help Jackie the variety manager build the Boxing Day display on Christmas Eve. We had been at it for hours. Every time we thought we were done another trailer showed up at the door with more product. By 8:30, Jackie was at her breaking point. The tears started flowing as she thought Christmas wasn't going to happen for her this year. Murray (without consulting me) said, "Jackie, get out of here. Dave and I can finish this up in thirty minutes." Witnessing the relief on her face and the tears of sadness turning into tears of joy was worth Murray and I staying for an additional three hours. I did have a brief discussion with Murray about the finer points of productivity...the first one being, "The more the merrier."

◊ ◊ ◊

I was a first assistant when the company president was in our store and asked me how my life was. "Dave, have you got anyone special in your life? Are you thinking of marriage and having a family?" I replied, "I'm about as single as can be right now." A very sad, almost disturbed expression came over the president's face. He then asked the second assistant, "Jim, how about you?" "Well sir," Jim replied, "I have been seeing a young lady for about six months now and we're discussing a possible spring wedding." The president, his face now beaming with anticipation, said, "That's great, Jim, family is so important." The president left and I turned to Jim. "You're not seeing anyone!" Jim simply replied, "After seeing his reaction to your answer, I decided I better give him the answer he wants!"

I was in grade twelve and wanted to play basketball for my high school, as I had the previous two years. I asked Harry (the assistant) if I could work only Wednesdays and Saturdays for the next four months. It didn't seem like a problem until I saw the next schedule; I worked Monday, Tuesday, Thursday, and Friday. When I saw Harry, I said, "Harry, I must have explained the time I require off wrong." Harry replied, "No, I understand. You better make a choice: basketball or the store." Harry added, "Will you ever make money playing basketball?" I then confessed, "Well, I'm actually what you would call a 'two and twenty' player. If there's two minutes left and we were up by twenty points or down by twenty points, I would get to play." After a very long and painful searching of my soul, I decided that I would fill grocery baskets for money and fill the other kind of baskets in my spare time, just for fun.

◊ ◊ ◊

As a merchant you try to capture as much sales as possible. I would often challenge the department managers to take risks. If they got caught with too much inventory, at least we know we sold as much as possible. One day I was discussing selection and production of product with the bakery manager. I asked, "Where are the bar cakes?" He confidently replied, "I don't make them any more – they sell too quick!"

◊ ◊ ◊

Every store has a safety committee, and part of their responsibility was to do two fire drills each year. They chose the day and informed the local fire department and myself. At 7:30 am on a very cold Tuesday morning in February, the drill began. We had about ninety-five employees in the store to participate in the exercise. The alarm went and the people reacted. Doors were closed, exits were opened, and people made their way to the meeting point outside. The department managers had the schedules to ensure everyone was accounted for. After several high fives and pats on the back we returned to the store, to find three of the contracted floor crew running around in a panic not understanding what was happening. I thought to myself, three lost out of ninety-eight isn't too bad.

Looking Back

As I read through these stories, I found myself questioning if I accomplished what I had originally intended. As I stated in my prologue, I was hoping to inform the public about this dynamic industry and give its employees the respect they deserve. I believe that the stories reflected typical everyday situations and how they were handled in the store. Whether the employees gained a greater respect, only you can answer that question.

Writing this book gave me the opportunity to look back over my time in the industry. I began to question, was it all worth it? Working fifty-five to sixty hours a week and working evenings and weekends had caused many of us to miss out on a normal life. Our schedule never matched the eight to five Monday to Friday that the rest of the world worked. Our days were filled with events that challenged us, never history making, but also never the same. The need to make quality decisions quickly was essential. Multi-tasking became part of our lifestyle. It was extremely difficult separating the store and home life. Many marriages ended and some never got started. I haven't met someone who understands just how demanding this career is, who isn't involved themselves. Many of the relationships I had with people outside the industry simply saw me as a person who put canned beans on the shelf. Oddly enough whenever we, inside the industry tried to make the job too complicated, I was often the one to remind everyone, "We just sell beans."

Had I written this book to somehow justify my thirty-one years in the grocery industry? That thought lasted only a few seconds. I loved what I was doing and I didn't need the book to remind me of that. Isn't it typical that you don't realize what motivates you to do something until you aren't doing it anymore? I wonder just how much more effective we would be if we understood why we chose a particular direction while we're still travelling that direction.

Perhaps I wished to be publicly recognized for my efforts over the years. I've witnessed other people with that desire and found it not very becoming. I always thought I only needed to know in my heart if I was doing a good job.

Then I started to consider the possibility that this book could be my legacy — this is how I will be remembered. I also realized how fortunate it was that I wrote the book. This is my version of how these events took place and would be recorded for posterity. As I continued to read, it occurred to me that most of these stories were not about the industry but about the interaction between people in this industry. These stories told about how teams were built, how obstacles were overcome and, most importantly, how friendships were forged.

I realize that I am possibly over thinking this, but you write this many stories about your life and tell me you wouldn't become reflective and soul searching. I soon came to see the truth. The book is not my legacy. "*Walk an Aisle in My Shoes*" actually is a reminder of what or who my legacy actually is: all the people that allowed me to be part of their lives and who shared a part of themselves with me. I am very proud to have played a role in this industry and forever grateful for the people it allowed me to know. To all the people who shared a part of themselves with me, all I can say is thank you.

Some may view their life like the path of a ship cutting through the ocean, leaving the water swirling and churned up by the propellers, its wake rocking everything it comes into contact with. When I look back over my life and career, I hope to see what a farmer would see looking behind his plough: leaving a path that allows for the planting of ideas and the growth of individuals. If this book captured even a part of that I'll be satisfied.

About the Author

Dave Rackham was born during the summer of 1958 in North Vancouver, B.C. In 1972, his family was transferred to Saskatoon, then Regina, before finally settling in Calgary. A true westerner, Dave learned to spin a tale early in life. A thirty-year career in the grocery industry fueled this talent, and with the encouragement of friends and co-workers, Dave put his stories to paper. Blessed with an incredible memory (according to Dave) and the ability to see humour in most any situation, he wrote his first book *Walk an Aisle in My Shoes.*